T0247072

The
Leadership
Style of
Jesus

The Leadership Style of Jesus

Michael Youssef

HARVEST HOUSE PUBLISHERS
EUGENE, OREGON

Published in association with the literary agency of Wolgemuth & Associates. Inc.

Cover design by Studio Gearbox
Cover images © Artistdesign.13 / Shutterstock
Interior design by Chad Dougherty

For bulk, special sales, or ministry purchases, please call 1-800-547-8979.
Email: CustomerService @hhpbooks. com

The Leadership Style of Jesus

Copyright © 2013 by Michael Youssef
Published by Harvest House Publishers
Eugene, Oregon 97408
www.harvesthousepublishers.com

ISBN 97 8-0-7369-9015-8 (pbk)
ISBN 97 8-A-7369-9016-5 (eBook)

The Library of Congress has cataloged the edition as follows:

Library of Congress Cataloging-in-Publication Data
Youssef, Michael.
    The leadership style of Jesus / Michael Youssef.
        pages cm
    ISBN 978-0-7369-5230-9 (pbk.)
    ISBN 978-0-7369-5231-6 (eBook)
    1. Leadership—Religious aspects—Christianity. 2. Jesus Christ—Example. I. Title.
    BV4597.53.L43Y68 2013
    253—dc23

                                                                    2013007367

Printed in the United States of America

24 25 26 27 28 29 29 30 / BP / 10 9 8 7 6 5 4 3 2 1

To my wife, Elizabeth,
and my children, Sarah, Natasha,
Joshua, and Jonathan

Acknowledgments

I wrote an abbreviated version of this book back in 1986. Since then it has been read by millions around the world in twelve of the world's most spoken languages.

I am confident that this expanded and much enlarged book will help many leaders and aspiring leaders to follow in the leadership style of Jesus, the greatest leader who ever lived.

For this I want to thank Harvest House Publishers for their vision and the diligence of Wolgemuth and Associates. Above all, I want to thank my very able compiler and editor, Jim Denney.

Contents

Part 1: The Beginnings of Leadership

1. The Need to Be Confirmed 11
2. Acknowledging Those Who Have
   Gone Before 21

Part 2: The Qualities of Leadership

3. The Leader as Shepherd 31
4. Man's Rules Versus God's Principles 45
5. Courage 53
6. Gentleness 63
7. Generosity 71
8. Truthfulness 79
9. Forgiveness 87

Part 3: The Temptations of Leadership

10. Power 99
11. Ego 115
12. Anger 121

Part 4: The Problems of Leadership

13. The Lonely Calling 133
14. Doubters 145
15. Criticism 153
16. Molehills and Mountains 167

Part 5: The Future of Leadership

17. Where Leaders Come From 177
18. Turning Followers into Leaders 187

    Notes 199

Part 1

The
Beginnings
of Leadership

1

The Need to Be Confirmed

A friend once gave a talk to a group of children. Robed like a character from Bible times, he said, "I have something to tell you—something I've never told anyone else before." He pulled open the robe to reveal a big *S* on his T-shirt. "Kids," he said, "I'm Superman!"

The children laughed. One child called out, "If you're Superman, fly up to the ceiling!"

My friend went on to explain that many people make claims about who they are, but not everyone can offer proof. "The problem," he said, "is that once I tell you I'm Superman, I have to prove it."

Leadership works the same way. Whenever anyone says "I'm a leader," that person will be put to the test. He or she must back that claim with proof. What kind of proof? Well, the most obvious kind of proof that a person is a leader is that he or she has *followers*. If you don't have followers, you are not a leader.

Followers are people who believe in you and trust you enough to follow in your footsteps. They endorse your leadership by saying to you, "I recognize your leadership ability. I trust you. I want to be like you. I want to learn from you. I want to go where you lead me."

A leader is, by definition, a person who works through other people to achieve a goal or a vision. A president sets a vision or direction for the nation, then commissions his staff and his cabinet to achieve that vision, works with Congress to enact that vision, and inspires the citizenry to embrace that vision. A corporate CEO casts a vision for the company, works through the management team to implement that vision, and motivates the workforce to fulfill that vision at every level. A pastor articulates a biblically based vision for the church, and works through the church board, the elders and deacons, the teachers and youth workers and volunteers, and all the members to transform that vision into Christ-centered ministry.

The ultimate role model of effective leadership is Jesus Christ. During his earthly ministry, Jesus worked through people to achieve the vision called "the kingdom of heaven." He began by calling to himself a circle of twelve people from assorted temperaments and backgrounds, including fishermen (Simon, Andrew, James, and John), antigovernment political extremists (Simon the Zealot and Judas Iscariot), and a pro-government collaborator (Matthew the tax collector). Jesus mentored these followers, taught them and challenged them, and united them into a unified force focused on a single goal. Then he pushed them out of their comfort zones and delegated important tasks to them, and ultimately founded his church through them.

Jesus worked through the Twelve to establish a church that has endured for two millennia and now circles the globe. Jesus inspired trust and followership in the people he met. As they followed and watched his life, they became witnesses, confirming that he truly was the Messiah—the leader promised in the Old Testament, anointed by God, descended from David, and sent to save his people.

Jesus also shared his vision with a wider circle of disciples and with the masses, and he inspired confidence and enthusiasm about his vision of a coming kingdom. In the process of casting his kingdom vision and teaching in parables, he enabled people to see his vision for themselves, and he drew many people to his vision. Jesus the Messiah created a community of people who were focused on his kingdom vision, and by leading, teaching, motivating, and inspiring those people, he changed the world.

As we see in John's gospel, Jesus offered seven basic proofs, seven distinct confirmations that he was truly the Messiah, God's anointed leader. After we examine those seven proofs, we will see how to apply the lessons of the leadership style of Jesus to every leadership arena—governments and corporations, churches and schools, military units and sports teams, and the most intimate leadership arena of all, the home.

First Witness: The Father

The first proof Jesus offers to confirm his leadership role is the witness of God the Father. He told his hearers, "And the Father who sent me has himself borne witness about me" (John 5:37a). What did Jesus mean? He was speaking about the Father's stamp of approval—an affirmation that God issued publicly, immediately after Jesus was baptized by John the Baptist. In Matthew's gospel we read:

> And when Jesus was baptized, immediately he went up from the water, and behold, the heavens were opened to him, and he saw the Spirit of God descending like a dove and coming to rest on him; and behold, a voice from heaven said, "This is my beloved Son, with whom I am well pleased" (Matthew 3:16-17).

In the presence of John the Baptist and many other witnesses, God the Father openly announced his eternal relationship between himself and Jesus of Nazareth. Here we see a stark contrast between Jesus and every other so-called "messiah" who claims to come in the name of God. For example, Joseph Smith, the founder of Mormonism, claimed he was all alone at night on a wooded hill when he was visited by an angel; that angel, he said, revealed a new religion to him out of a book of golden plates. Muhammad, the founder of Islam, supposedly entered Jerusalem by night and claimed to hear the voice of God speak to him while he was alone.

Go through the history of various religions and you hear repeated claims of "in the middle of the night, when no one else was around, God spoke to me." But Jesus did not have to make unverified claims of a revelation by night. God the Father openly confirmed his Son as the anointed Messiah.

On a less public occasion, Jesus took his three closest disciples, his executive committee as it were, to a mountain (later known as the Mount of Transfiguration). What these three disciples witnessed that night is recorded in Mark's gospel:

> And after six days Jesus took with him Peter and James and John, and led them up a high mountain by them-selves. And he was transfigured before them, and his clothes became radiant, intensely white, as no one on earth could bleach them. And there appeared to them Elijah with Moses, and they were talking with Jesus. And Peter said to Jesus, "Rabbi, it is good that we are here. Let us make three tents, one for you and one for Moses and one for Elijah." For he did not know what to say, for they were terrified. And a cloud overshadowed them, and a voice came out of the cloud, "This is my beloved Son; listen to him." And suddenly, looking around, they no longer saw anyone with them but Jesus only (Mark 9:2-8).

The messiahship of Jesus was confirmed as Jesus conversed with Elijah and Moses, and as the voice of God said, "This is my beloved Son." Jesus was not a self-proclaimed, self-anointed leader. His right to be called Jesus the Messiah was proclaimed by God the Father, and that proclamation was heard by many witnesses.

Second Witness: John the Baptist

The opening chapter of John's gospel reveals the testimony of a second witness, John the Baptist:

> And John bore witness: "I saw the Spirit descend from heaven like a dove, and it remained on him. I myself did not know him, but he who sent me to baptize with water said to me, 'He on whom you see the Spirit descend and remain, this is he who baptizes with the Holy Spirit.' And I have seen and have borne witness that this is the Son of God" (John 1:32-34).

As Jesus later said of John the Baptist, "You sent to John, and he has borne witness to the truth" (John 5:33). John the Baptist, who called himself "the voice of one crying out in the wilderness," was a forerunner and a witness for Jesus, a man sent by God with a unique ministry to confirm to the world the identity of Jesus the Messiah.

Third Witness: Jesus Himself

It may seem strange that Jesus called himself to the witness stand to testify to his own ministry as God's anointed Messiah. But after referring to the confirming witness of his Father and John the Baptist, Jesus said, "But the testimony that I have is greater than that of John. For the works that the Father has given me to accomplish, the very works that I am doing, bear witness about me that the Father has sent me" (John 5:36).

Later, Jesus said, "I and the Father are one" (John 10:30). His hearers understood exactly what he was saying, and they picked up stones to stone him to death. They justified their intention to kill him, saying, "It is not for a good work that we are going to stone you but for blasphemy, because you, being a man, make yourself God" (John 10:33). On another occasion, Jesus told the people that because they had seen him, they had seen God the Father (see John 14:7).

Jesus didn't merely *claim* to have a unique and eternal relationship with God. Everything about his life backed up this claim. Through the evidence of his life, Jesus made it clear that he was a leader to be followed.

Fourth Witness: The Holy Spirit

As we have already noted, the Holy Spirit gave his blessing and confirmation at the baptism of Jesus by descending on him like a dove and remaining on him. Even though the story is presented to us beautifully, in symbolic language, there are undoubtedly depths to the witness of the Spirit in the life of Jesus that we don't fully comprehend. But we do know that the Holy Spirit confirmed the ministry and leadership of the Lord Jesus. The presence of the Spirit gave Jesus the authority to preach the gospel and perform a variety of miracles.

Fifth Witness: Scripture

The Old Testament confirmed the leadership of Jesus. Prophets foretold his coming, his messianic ministry, and his death. Some of the most explicit prophecies about Jesus were written by the prophet Isaiah. He pictured the birth of Jesus (Isaiah 9:6), the suffering of Jesus (Isaiah 53:4-10), the servanthood of Jesus (Isaiah 42:1-4), and even the announcement of Jesus by John the Baptist (Isaiah 40:3). Many other messianic passages, such as Psalms 22, 69, 110, and 118, speak vividly of Jesus's life, ministry, lordship, rejection by Israel, death, and resurrection.

As the Lord Jesus told the corrupt religious leaders who persecuted him, "You search the Scriptures because you think that in them you have eternal life; and it is they that bear witness about me, yet you refuse to come to me that you may have life" (John 5:39-40).

Sixth Witness: Miracles

The ministry of Jesus was confirmed by the miracles he performed. John's gospel refers to them as "signs." Though John cites fewer miracles than any of the other gospel writers, the signs he mentions bear witness to the purpose, power, and leadership authority of Jesus.

It's important to understand that Jesus did not perform these signs as an act of showmanship. An attention-seeking showman would have performed magic tricks to amaze and attract the crowds. Jesus often performed his most amazing miracles quietly, out of public view, and he frequently told witnesses to tell no one. His reluctance to perform miracles in order to play to the crowd confirms his words, "I do not receive glory from people" (John 5:41).

Seventh Witness: The Disciples

The disciples traveled with Jesus throughout his earthly ministry. They saw what he did, heard his teachings, and believed. When the religious leaders persecuted Jesus and he spoke openly of the hardship of following him, many would-be disciples turned away. Only a few continued to follow him.

Those who persevered with Christ included Simon Peter, who said, "Lord, to whom shall we go? You have the words of eternal life" (John 6:68). In saying that, Peter didn't merely mean that Jesus knew the rules of life or could explain how life should be lived; he meant that Jesus himself was the Source and Giver of eternal life.

The author of the gospel of John was himself a follower of Jesus. In the next to last verse of his gospel, John says, "This is the disciple who is bearing witness about these things, and who has written these things, and we know that his testimony is true" (John 21:24).

Today's Leaders

We who are involved in leadership today can hardly claim to possess the unique qualifications of Jesus the Messiah. But by observing his life, we learn this important leadership principle: *The call to leadership must be confirmed.*

What if someone walked into your office and said, "I have come to lead you into truth"? First, such an approach would be so strange that you'd probably call security to have that person removed.

But suppose something about this person's manner made you want to examine his claims. How would you know who he was? How would you test the validity of his claim? How would you know if this person could lead you to the truth or not? You would undoubtedly ask a few reasonable questions: "By what right or authority do you speak? What are your qualifications or credentials? Could I see your résumé? Do you have any references?"

A person cannot simply come out of nowhere and expect to be followed as a leader. A leader must prove himself or herself competent to lead. This is true whether one is a leader in the religious realm or the secular realm.

A pastor of a church must overcome a number of hurdles to achieve a position of leadership. Normally, a pastor is first trained, then ordained (formally recognized as someone called by God as a spiritual leader). Anyone can *train* for leadership, but only God *calls* people to spiritual leadership. Pastors generally serve apprenticeships that allow them to grow into leadership, to become intellectually, emotionally, and spiritually more mature. Throughout this process, church leaders and members have an opportunity to observe and recognize the pastor's unique gifts and abilities.

Authentic spiritual leaders are also confirmed by people outside the church. The apostle Paul, when giving instructions to his protégé, Timothy, on the subject of ordination, said that an authentic spiritual leader "must be well thought of by outsiders, so that he may not fall into disgrace, into a snare of the devil" (1 Timothy 3:7).

This rule of confirmation applies in secular leadership settings as well. Whether in business, government, the military, academia, or even the home, people must earn the right to lead. I may believe that I have been divinely appointed to head Apple Computer, but if I walked into Apple headquarters in Cupertino, California, and announced, "I'm here to take over," I assure you they would not usher me into the CEO's office. Most likely, I would be ushered to the parking lot.

If I would like to become the CEO of a major corporation, I will have to go through a process of confirmation. I will have to start at the bottom and be patient. I'll have to listen, learn, be mentored and instructed, demonstrate initiative and creativity, acquire skills, make friends and influential connections, and gradually move up the corporate ladder. At each level of my career, some individual—or more likely, a group of individuals—will have to examine my work, assess my character, and say, "Yes, he's ready. He has earned a chance to move up to the next level."

Many would-be leaders lack the patience to climb that ladder. Full of hubris and the arrogance of youth, they don't even know how much they don't know. So they vainly insist that they have what it takes to lead.

I have learned over the years how to separate in the interview stage the leadership contenders from the pretenders. The most obvious sign of a pretender is a candidate who tells you that your organization is desperate for someone with his ability and he will save your organization. That kind of arrogance is always a red light.

I remember one candidate for ministry who was turned down by a church and told to wait until he had gained more experience and maturity. His embittered response: "You are going against God's will." The people on the committee were all friends of his. They wanted the best for him. But they were also committed to confirming God's call on his life, and at that point, they simply could not do so in good conscience. They saw too many character flaws in this man, and his impatient and prideful reply only confirmed that they were right about him.

I have also seen, in both the Christian and secular worlds, people who looked great on paper, who had impressive résumés, but who proved incapable of leading once they were hired and placed in the hot seat. They didn't have the aptitude to lead, and they lacked the confirmation of other people.

All authentic leaders must be confirmed in order to lead. This brings us to the first leadership principle we learn from the life of Jesus:

Principle 1

Even Jesus received confirmation as a leader.
We too must be confirmed as leaders.

2 Acknowledging Those Who Have Gone Before

At the 2009 Tony Awards ceremony, various actors, playwrights, producers, and other luminaries of Broadway went to the platform to receive their awards. Most would take a few moments to acknowledge the various people who made that moment possible, from Broadway colleagues to seventh-grade drama teachers.

But one actor took a different approach with his acceptance speech. "There are so many people that I really could thank," said comedian Martin Short, "but I won't. Because the reality is, I did it all myself!"

Martin Short was joking, and the line got a big laugh. But his words remind us of a very real danger for those of us in leadership today—the danger of pride, the danger of believing we deserve all the credit for our successes. We begin to think, *I'm so brilliant! Look at what I accomplished all by myself!*

In truth, no one achieves anything alone. And this is especially true of leaders. After all, a leader achieves goals by working through other people. Every great leader is a product of his or her teachers, mentors, and other influences. And every great leader gets things done by delegating responsibility to others, especially the people on the front lines of the organization.

When a leader begins to think, *I did it all myself*, that leader is in big trouble.

On the Shoulders of Giants

I will always remember what one of my professors said: "When you do research, pay special attention to the one or two names that keep coming up as references. Those people probably laid the groundwork in that field. Others built on their foundation—or tried to make a reputation for themselves by opposing their work. Even the opposition had to acknowledge the achievements of those who laid the groundwork."

The willingness to acknowledge those who went before is a characteristic of good leadership. Great leaders are secure enough to give credit where credit is due. They honestly and readily admit, "I could not have done it alone." As the renowned English physicist Sir Isaac Newton (1642–1727) once said, "If I have seen farther than other men, it is because I have stood on the shoulders of giants."

When I earned my PhD, I realized it was hardly an individual achievement. I received help from many people in order to achieve that goal.

First, I owed a debt of gratitude to my godly mother who raised me in the Christian faith, who prayed for me daily, and who taught me the importance of prayer. She built into my life many of the character qualities I needed to stay motivated and focused on that goal, including traits of perseverance, hard work, and faith in God.

At age twenty-one, I emigrated from Egypt to Sydney, Australia. I arrived in Sydney as a stranger, knowing only one couple, and I knew them only by name and reputation. I also had a letter of introduction to Anglican Canon D.W.B. Robinson, later Archbishop of Sydney. Archbishop Robinson encouraged me and supported me as I struggled to study and learn effectively in a new culture. Without his encouragement, I would not have been able to study at Moore Theological College.

Then I met John Haggai. His confidence in me enabled me to believe in God's call on my life. When I was thirty-one, he asked me to head the Haggai Institute, a worldwide ministry with offices on six continents. Working in that position enabled me to acquire what seemed like fifty years' worth of maturity in just eight years. By God's grace, I was able to lead the organization, study for my doctorate, and write books all at the same time.

All the while I had my most trusted partner, my wife, Elizabeth, who gave me love, support, and encouragement. Whenever I traveled overseas or stayed up late to study, she took over the roles of *both* parents to our four children.

And there were so many other giants in my life, too many to mention. Standing on their shoulders, I felt there was nothing I couldn't do. I owe so much to all of them, and I will never forget their impact on my life and ministry.

Mentors and Forerunners

Jesus told his disciples that the fields were ready to harvest. He used the fields as a metaphor to describe a state of spiritual readiness and openness on the part of the people all around them. The people were ready to receive the gospel, the good news of the kingdom. Jesus went on to say:

> "Already the one who reaps is receiving wages and gathering fruit for eternal life, so that sower and reaper may rejoice together. For here the saying holds true, 'One sows and another reaps.' I sent you to reap that for which you did not labor. Others have labored, and you have entered into their labor" (John 4:36-38).

Jesus wanted his disciples to know that they owed a debt of gratitude to all those who labored before them. He could easily have reminded them that the very land they stood on had been won in combat centuries earlier by Joshua and the faithful Israelites. He could have mentioned the rabbis and other leaders who kept the Jewish faith and taught the people.

When the apostle Paul wrote to the Corinthians, he had a similar idea in mind. The Corinthians had begun to divide into factions, elevating certain leaders they liked and aligning themselves with those leaders. Some even called themselves followers of Paul. So Paul wrote to them:

> What then is Apollos? What is Paul? Servants through whom you believed, as the Lord assigned to each. I planted, Apollos watered, but God gave the growth. So neither he who plants nor he who waters is anything, but only God who gives the growth. He who plants and he who waters are one, and each will receive his wages according to his labor. For we are God's fellow workers. You are God's field, God's building (1 Corinthians 3:5-9).

Jesus became a leader, the anointed Messiah, *only* after John the Baptist had prepared the way. The apostle Peter became a leader among the disciples and later a leader in the church, but he became part of the Lord's circle of disciples *only* after his brother Andrew invited him to follow the Lord with him.

You will never meet a self-made leader, a leader who has pulled himself up by his bootstraps. Every true leader is a product of the parenting, teaching, coaching, mentoring, and guiding that has gone before. Every leader stands on the shoulders of giants. This is true both in the religious realm and in the secular world. As Tom Morris observed in *If Aristotle Ran General Motors*, "Socrates had a student named Plato, Plato had a student named Aristotle, and Aristotle had a student named Alexander the Great."[1] Behind every great leader stand generations of giants.

An Attitude of Interdependence

Why did Jesus, after training and instructing his followers, send them out two by two (see Luke 10:1)? One obvious reason is that there is safety in numbers. Two people working and traveling together can encourage each other and help each other when they visit unfamiliar places. Yet Jesus may have had in mind an equally important but less obvious reason.

Might Peter have come back after visiting a city all by himself, saying, "Look what I did"? Could it be that Jesus wanted to teach his disciples that they needed to depend on one another and on him? He may have wanted to help the disciples to understand that they were all part of one body in Christ—a theme that would appear repeatedly in the writings of the apostle Paul (see Romans 12:3-8 and 1 Corinthians 12:12).

Jesus himself had the right to take credit for everything from creation onward. Yet he exemplified the humility of the servant. Jesus could have pointed out the flaws and failures of those who went before him: "You think Abraham was great? Remember, he had his share of failings. And Moses? Don't forget all the times he got angry and disobeyed God. And don't forget how Abraham feared Pharaoh so much that he lied and said Sarah was his sister! If you want to know what real greatness is, look at me!"

But Jesus was not driven (as so many leaders are today) by the need to receive credit, applause, and attention. Jesus acknowledged those who went before him, including Abraham (see John 8:53) and Moses (see John 5:45-46). If we want to follow the leadership style of Jesus Christ, we must acknowledge others in the same Christlike way that he did. Here are some thoughts that may help you to maintain a humble, Christlike attitude toward your own leadership role.

1. *All ability, including leadership ability, is a gift from God.* John the Baptist said it best: "A person cannot receive even one thing unless it is given him from heaven" (John 3:27). John knew he did not send himself as the Lord's forerunner; God had chosen him, prepared him, and endowed him with the ability to prepare the way for the Messiah. The leadership ability we have is a gift from God—and it should humble us to recognize this all-important truth.

When the apostle Paul wrote about spiritual gifts in 1 Corinthians 12 and elsewhere, he acknowledged the same principle. No matter what spiritual gifts we may have, they all came from God. We cannot invent spiritual gifts, nor can we bestow spiritual gifts on ourselves.

2. *We can do nothing to earn our leadership abilities.* You cannot earn a gift. Spiritual gifts are given to us by the grace of our sovereign God. We can improve certain skills. We can polish our public speaking ability. We can learn to become more effective administrators. We can practice more efficient time management. But the calling to be a leader and the essential ability to achieve a vision through people is a gift from God.

3. *Leadership ability is no reason to boast.* God gives leadership ability to some, and to others he gives the ability to recognize and follow leaders. Some people have gifted hands. Others have gifted voices. Others have gifted minds. Who, then, has a reason to boast of his or her gifts? Is the leader greater than the follower? What can the leader accomplish without gifted followers? Nothing! Everything the leader is, has, and does comes from God, so no leader has any reason to boast of his leadership ability.

4. *We should give thanks to God for our leadership abilities.* Since God is the source of our leadership gifts, we should be grateful. He gave us our natural talents and spiritual gifts. He brought parents, mentors, teachers, coaches, and other influential people into our lives. He led us through experiences that sharpened our leadership skills. Have you thanked God for making you the leader you are today?

5. *We should acknowledge those who have helped us on our leadership journey.* Olympic athletes begin with outstanding natural talent, but natural talent is not enough. Every great athlete needs direction, instruction, and correction in order to transform natural talent into Olympic gold. Look at the life story of any Olympic champion, and you find parents who sacrificed, teachers who inspired, coaches who instructed, and teammates who motivated. Olympic competition, even in individual events, is a team effort. Olympic champions

almost always acknowledge the many people who made it possible for them to compete at that level. Leaders need to learn from the example of Olympians.

The following advertisement appeared some time ago in the *Wall Street Journal* with the headline, "Do You Remember Your First Break?" The ad read:

> Someone saw something in you once.
>
> That's partly why you are where you are today.
>
> It could have been a thoughtful parent, a perceptive teacher, a demanding drill sergeant, an appreciative employer, or just a friend who dug down in his pocket and came up with a few bucks.
>
> Whoever it was had the kindness and the foresight to bet on your future.
>
> Those are two beautiful qualities that separate the human being from the orangutan.
>
> In the next 24 hours, take 10 minutes to write a grateful note to the person that helped you.
>
> You'll keep a wonderful friendship alive.
>
> Matter of fact, take another 10 minutes to give somebody else a break.
>
> Who knows?
>
> Someday you might get a nice letter.
>
> It could be one of the most gratifying messages you ever read. [2]

As you read that text, I'm sure that God brought to mind specific people who gave you your first break, who encouraged and influenced you, who mentored you and impacted your life. Have you acknowledged and thanked the people who made you the leader you are today?

If you have great leadership ability, be humble and grateful, not prideful. Acknowledge and thank God who gave you your natural abilities and spiritual gifts. Don't forget to thank the giants on whose shoulders you stand. This brings us to the second leadership principle that comes from the life of Jesus:

Principle 2

Great leaders acknowledge
the giants who preceded them.

Part 2

The
Qualities
of Leadership

3

The Leader as Shepherd

had just finished having lunch with the chief executive officer of a large banking institution. As we walked out of the bank's executive dining room, we passed a suite of offices. The banker paused to say hello to the receptionist, asking about her husband who had recently been hospitalized. Later, as we stepped off the elevator, he greeted two bank employees by name. In the lobby of the bank, he paused and chatted with the guard, calling him by name and asking about his wife, also by name.

Hundreds of people must have worked in the bank's central office, yet the CEO knew the name of each one. I walked away amazed, not because he had such a good memory, but because he actually knew these people. They weren't just names on index cards, and he wasn't just pretending to care. He related to them as individuals, with distinct personalities, hopes and dreams, and problems.

It occurred to me that this banker was truly a "good shepherd" of his corporation. Whether consciously or subconsciously, he had patterned his leadership style after the One who said, "I am the good shepherd. I know my own and my own know me, just as the Father knows me and I know the Father; and I lay down my life for the sheep" (John 10:14-15).

By contrast, I once had an encounter with another leader, a very different kind of shepherd. One Sunday morning, I stood next to the pastor of a prestigious church at the conclusion of the worship service. He shook hands with all the parishioners as they filed by. He greeted each one with a bright smile and the cheery words, "How are you?"

On the surface, this pastor seemed to take a personal interest in each person, but in at least a dozen instances, I heard him say, "How are you? Ah, that's good," before the person could even reply. Then his hand would reach out for the next in line with the same smile and the same greeting.

I saw one elderly woman approach the pastor, and he said, "I hope you are doing well today."

The woman looked tired and sad, and she replied, "I had to call an ambulance for my husband Thursday night, and he is still in intensive care—"

"Yes," the pastor said. "It's so nice to see you this morning. It's always a joy to have you in the service." And his hand immediately reached out for the next person in line.

I could hardly believe what I had just witnessed. I felt embarrassed for this hurting woman, embarrassed for the pastor, and embarrassed for the church. As a visitor, I didn't want to interject myself between a pastor and a parishioner, but in my own small way, I tried to make up for the pastor's insensitivity to her need. "What is your husband's name?" I said, taking the woman's hand. "I'd like to remember him in prayer every day next week."

I don't want to judge this pastor harshly. I can easily understand that, with a large congregation, an overworked staff, and the heavy ministry load he carries, he probably could not focus. He might have been burdened by personal problems that day, or he might have felt anxious about an upcoming event. His seeming insensitivity may have been out of character for him.

But I left that church with an impression of that pastor quite different from the impression I got from the banker. The word *pastor* comes from the Latin word for "shepherd." Yet the banker knew his sheep better than the pastor knew his. The banker was more of an authentic shepherd than the "shepherd" was. Worst of all, I had the distinct impression that the pastor had other priorities.

When Jesus said, "I know my own...and I lay down my life for the sheep," he wasn't just saying that he knew their names. He was saying that he loves his sheep, serves his sheep, and sacrifices his own interests for the sake of his sheep. That is what a good shepherd does. That is how a shepherd-leader leads.

Loveless Shepherds?

Jesus, the Good Shepherd, said, "I know my own and my own know me." But a shepherd who does not love the sheep does not care to know the sheep as persons. To a shepherd who does not love, the sheep are just members. In many churches today they call them audiences. They are just employees on the payroll, a faceless set of statistics: "We had a 12 percent increase in church membership this year," or "Our work force was 6 percent more productive this year."

Our society places a great emphasis on numbers. TV programs, radio shows, and even Internet sites are judged by the size of their audience, and advertising revenues rise or fall based on those numbers. The value of a corporation or stock is determined by numbers, such as price to earnings ratio (P/E), earnings per share (EPS), market capitalization, and so forth. And even churches are sometimes judged on numbers, such as the increase (or decline) of membership or donations.

This focus on numbers, while understandable, can be misleading and even harmful. An excellent television drama series about important social issues may lose in the ratings to a mindless reality show that subtracts from our cultural IQ. An excellent but undervalued corporation may struggle because it is underestimated and undervalued. And a church may become wildly successful (by the world's standards) by preaching an unbiblical feel-good gospel, while God does his real work through a struggling storefront church where the shepherd knows his sheep.

The leadership style of Jesus is not focused on statistics. It's based on love. The leader who practices shepherd-leadership knows his sheep personally and cares about them individually. His love for the sheep is not an abstract idea or empty slogan. He and his fellow shepherds know each member of the flock, and the flock knows them.

How do Jesus's sheep know him? They don't know him merely intellectually. They don't merely understand certain facts about him. They know him intimately and personally, because they sense the shepherd-love that radiates from him. As one of his sheep, I may experience doubts and fears. But when I see my shepherd, my fears melt away. I know my shepherd, I trust his leadership ability, and I know he cares for me.

Consider the sheep and shepherds of Jesus's day. Shepherds in ancient Palestine put the safety of their sheep ahead of their own safety. In the Old Testament, the young shepherd David fought and killed a lion with his bare hands because the predator had come to attack his sheep. By understanding this deep level of commitment that shepherds had for their flocks, we can better understand the metaphor Jesus used when he called himself the Good Shepherd.

The Good Shepherd even lays down his life for the sheep. Jesus quoted Zechariah 13:7 when he predicted his death to his disciples. He said, "You will all fall away because of me this night. For it is written, 'I will strike the shepherd, and the sheep of the flock will be scattered'" (Matthew 26:31). When the Good Shepherd was struck down, he ensured the safety of his sheep. He willingly sacrificed his own life to save the sheep.

You may be accustomed to thinking of a leader as the person in the ivory tower, the corner office, the apex of the pyramid. In the traditional top-down leadership model, the leader remains aloof from the followers.

It's true that leaders must lead. Leaders must cast the vision, set the direction, inspire and motivate, and give orders. However, the leadership style of Jesus shows us that a leader does much more than that. A true shepherd-leader knows, serves, and sacrifices for the sheep.

Most leaders want to be the boss. Jesus says that a leader is called to serve. Most leaders want to give orders. Jesus says that a leader lays down his life for the sheep.

Shepherds Keep Moving

Wise shepherds constantly lead their sheep to greener pastures and greater opportunities. As the Twenty-Third Psalm tells us,

> The LORD is my shepherd; I shall not want.
>> He makes me lie down in green pastures.
> He leads me beside still waters.
>> He restores my soul.
> He leads me in paths of righteousness
>> for his name's sake.
> Even though I walk through the valley of the shadow
>> of death,
> I will fear no evil,
> for you are with me;
>> your rod and your staff,
>> they comfort me.
>
> (Psalm 23:1-4)

Good shepherd-leaders guide their sheep toward still waters, away from the turbulence of divisiveness. When the sheep stumble and fall, good shepherd-leaders use the shepherd's staff to comfort the sheep—not to goad them or beat them. Bosses control the sheep by inflicting fear; wise shepherds guide and comfort the sheep.

In 1987, a former Xerox sales manager, Howard Schultz, purchased a 3-store coffeehouse chain called Starbucks. When Starbucks made its initial public stock offering in 1992, the company had grown to 165 coffee shops. Today, there are more than 20,000 Starbucks outlets worldwide.

In 2000, Schultz pulled back from daily operations, resigning as CEO while continuing as chairman of the board. In 2008, Starbucks failed to anticipate a shrinking market for its wares as the global economy took a sharp turn for the worse. Increased competition from rival coffeehouse chains and even McDonald's, plus changes in coffee-drinking habits, had thrown Starbucks into a crisis. So Howard Schultz came back as CEO, hoping to turn the company around. It wasn't easy. As he told *Harvard Business Review*:

> When I returned in January 2008, things were actually worse than I'd thought...The decisions we had to make were very difficult, but first there had to be a time when we stood up in front of the entire company as leaders and made almost a confession—that the leadership had failed the 180,000 Starbucks people and their families. And even though I wasn't the CEO [when the crisis began], I had been around as chairman; I should have known more. I am responsible.

Some voices within the company said that Starbucks should abandon the values that had made the company successful. There was pressure to close down company-owned shops, franchise the Starbucks brand, and allow the people-first culture of Starbucks to become a thing of the past. Some urged a cost-saving compromise in the quality of the coffee beans they roasted.

It was clear that Starbucks would have to change—but Howard Schultz was determined to keep Starbucks values the same, especially its humanitarian values. He decided to take a big risk by holding the company's annual convention of store managers in New Orleans, a city that was still rebuilding after Hurricane Katrina. Most importantly, Starbucks would roll up its sleeves and help rebuild.

During the convention, Starbucks managers fanned out into

the city, investing fifty-four thousand volunteer hours and one million dollars of corporate money in community improvement projects. Starbucks employees helped restore neighborhoods, repaint buildings, and build new playgrounds in the hardest-hit sections of the city.

"If we hadn't had New Orleans," Schultz reflected, "we wouldn't have turned things around. It was real, it was truthful, and it was about leadership…We reinvested in our people, we reinvested in innovation, and we reinvested in the values of the company." The New Orleans convention marked the renaissance of Starbucks as a forward-thinking, people-focused company.[1]

Great leaders and organizations need to stay flexible and keep moving forward without abandoning their values. Great leaders know how to care for people, while also being nimble and responsive to change in the marketplace. Authentic leaders know how to keep moving forward without leaving willing followers behind.

Jesus, in his final words to his followers, expressed this principle well when he said, "Go therefore and make disciples of all nations, baptizing them in the name of the Father and of the Son and of the Holy Spirit, teaching them to observe all that I have commanded you. And behold, I am with you always, to the end of the age" (Matthew 28:19-20).

"Go," Jesus said. The church is an organization on the move—but it is also an organization that tries to pull everyone along. "I am with you always," Jesus says. As the church moves forward, we continue to focus on individuals and their needs. We continue to maintain our caring, our compassion, and our intimate sense of community. We are on the move, but wherever we go, Jesus, our Shepherd-Leader, goes with us.

The Visionary Shepherd

Jesus had a plan of action for his followers. He never intended for them to remain huddled in a small group in Jerusalem. His church would be a community in motion. Unfortunately, his followers either didn't understand his Great Commission or they weren't prepared to obey it right away. As the book of Acts records, the disciples stayed in and around Jerusalem. In fact, they might have been content to remain there forever. But the Good Shepherd wouldn't allow his flock to sit immobilized in one tiny corner of the Middle East.

Luke writes, "And there arose on that day a great persecution against the church in Jerusalem, and they were all scattered throughout the regions of Judea and Samaria, except the apostles" (Acts 8:1). What set the early church in motion? Persecution!

The early Christians might never have moved out and taken risks to spread the gospel had God not allowed persecution to prod them out of their comfort zone. Once the early Christians began to move, the Christian faith spread all over the civilized world. By AD 325, Christianity had become the official religion of the Roman Empire.

Authentic Christianity is a risk-taking faith, a daring adventure. When Jesus stood before his followers and gave them the Great Commission, he acted as the great Shepherd-Leader, the CEO of the Christian faith, unveiling a bold new venture, a radical new idea. "Go," he said. And after some initial reluctance, the church obeyed that commission and went into all the world. That is the leadership style of Jesus.

Leaders are people of vision. A leader sees a future no one else can see, and then takes his followers there.

In 1787, a British political leader named William Wilberforce gave his life to Christ. His conversion turned a spoiled, hedonistic, hard-drinking young gambler into a devout reformer. Wilberforce committed his life to ending the slave trade, even though all the political experts told him he was wasting his time. He waged a twenty-six-year political battle that resulted in passage of the Slave Trade Act of 1807, followed by the Slavery Abolition Act of 1833. Wilberforce saw what no one else could see, and then he turned his vision into reality.

Leaders of vision have an ability to look ahead and imagine a better, brighter future. The sheep can't see the vision that the shepherd sees. But the sheep trust the shepherd to lead them down the road, over the hill, to green pastures and refreshing waters.

Jesus had a vision that his followers could not see. It was a vision of a brighter future—but to get there, the shepherd would have to die, the sheep would have to scatter, and evil would appear to win. The pivotal verse in Luke's gospel reads: "When the days drew near for him to be taken up, he set his face to go to Jerusalem" (Luke 9:51). At this point in the gospel account, Jesus has just foretold his death to the disciples. He has reached a turning point on his way to realizing his vision. He has set his face to go to Jerusalem to be crucified.

The disciples didn't understand what Jesus was about to do. They came to a Samaritan village, and Jesus sent messengers into the village to make preparations for him to preach there. But the Samaritans would not receive him. So James and John, who were apparently very impressed with themselves, said, "Lord, do you want us to tell fire to come down from heaven and consume them?" But Jesus rebuked them and continued on his way toward Jerusalem, toward Calvary.

His disciples were blind to his vision, even though he had told them he was soon to be delivered into the hands of evil men to be killed. Jesus revealed his vision to his disciples, even though they did not understand it. He shared with them and prepared them as much as he could.

Through the example of Jesus, we see how important it is for leaders to be visionaries—yet leaders must be careful not to walk too far ahead of their followers. Like the Lord's disciples, your followers may not be able to see where you are leading them. But you must do what you can to share your vision with them and prepare them for the days ahead. A time will come when they will look back and remember what you told them, and it will all make sense.

As the visionary shepherd of your flock, you must always have the welfare of your sheep at heart. They should always feel that they are a part of your vision. If your followers begin to grumble, "Our leader is building his own little empire for the sake of his ego," then you have gotten too far ahead of your people. If they don't feel they have a stake in your vision, they won't be motivated to help you achieve it.

Jesus was not a private empire-builder. He had a vision of the kingdom, and everyone who follows him takes ownership of that vision and takes part in that kingdom.

The Balanced Shepherd-Leader

As leaders, we can't be everyone's best friend, but we can be available to our people. The people in your organization want to know if they can come to you with problems and questions. They want to know if your office door is open or closed to them. (I recently heard about one corporate leader who answered that question by taking the door off the hinges.) People want to know that you welcome their questions, ideas, and even their problems. You don't want to get into the habit of solving their problems for them, but you can teach them how to find the solutions for themselves.

One of the most successful open-door leaders in history was Walt Disney. He not only kept his door open, he walked around his studio and theme park, asking for opinions and ideas. He'd walk around Disneyland after closing time, talking to the ride operators, shop clerks, and security personnel, asking, "What are the customers saying about this attraction? How can we improve the experience for our customers? What problems do you see?"

Once, during a meeting with his Imagineers, the people who designed Disneyland attractions, he said, "See that janitor out in the hall? He has as many ideas as any of us." In the 1930s, he began posting the complete story layout of his cartoons on the studio walls. Anyone in the organization—from secretaries and typists to writers and animators—could offer suggestions. Disney paid a bonus for every idea that went into the finished cartoon.[2]

A shepherd-leader is never too busy to listen to the sheep and learn from them. At the same time, an effective leader maintains a balance in his relationships with the sheep so that all of his time isn't taken up dealing with complaints and problems. To be sure, a leader needs to spend the bulk of his time planning, goal-setting, decision-making, motivating, and leading his followers onward toward the vision. But in order for the organization to move forward, a leader also needs to avoid being sucked into the inertia that is a natural part of any organization. The effective shepherd-leader can often be heard saying, "Forward, march!" (though probably not in those exact words).

Jesus demonstrated this perfect balance in his leadership style. On the one hand, he promised his disciples that he would be present with them, and after he left, they would experience the presence and comfort of the Holy Spirit. But he also lifted the eyes of his disciples to the world and told them, "Go." Luke records Jesus's parting message to his disciples:

> "But you will receive power when the Holy Spirit has come upon you, and you will be my witnesses in Jerusalem and in all Judea and Samaria, and to the end of the earth" (Acts 1:8).

Notice the perfect balance of those words. Jesus promises the comfort and power of his Holy Spirit in their lives—and he also sends them out as his witnesses in Jerusalem, Judea and Samaria, and throughout the world. That is a key element of Christlike leadership—the balance between compassionate caring for the followers and effective motivation of the followers to move out and achieve the vision.

What Makes a Good Shepherd?

Growing up in the Middle East, I was able to observe first-hand the tender relationship between the sheep and the shepherd. In America and other Western countries, one must travel a long distance to see an actual shepherd at work. So you may find it hard to identify with the sheep-and-shepherd imagery that Jesus uses to explain his leadership style. But I have seen the sheep-and-shepherd relationship with my own eyes, and here's how the relationship works.

A good and faithful shepherd experiences a rewarding sense of satisfaction when he sees that his sheep are safe, well fed, and contented. He doesn't work merely to collect a paycheck. He spends his energies supplying the sheep with clear water for drinking and lush green pastures for grazing. Good shepherds spare no effort in providing shelter from bad weather. They constantly watch out for predators and keep the sheep free of parasites and diseases.

From dawn to dusk, the good shepherd selflessly dedicates his days to the welfare of his sheep. Even at night, a good shepherd sleeps with one eye open. He is ready to leap into action to protect his woolly followers at the first sign of trouble.

When Jesus claims to be the Good Shepherd, he is not using an empty metaphor. He is claiming to be a very special kind of leader—a leader who truly loves the flock and sacrifices himself for their benefit.

Many of the religious leaders in first-century Israel claimed to be shepherds of the nation and its people. Jesus saw through their hypocrisy, their corruption, and their arrogance. Jesus said, in effect, "I am not just a boss, ordering the sheep around, keeping the sheep in their place. I will never treat you with indifference or coldness, nor will I ever fail to return your calls. I am the shepherd, the guardian, the protector, the provider, and the companion of the sheep. I will lay down my life for you, and you can put your trust in me."

All responsibility for the safety and welfare of the sheep has been laid on his broad shoulders—and the sheep can trust the tenderness of the shepherd's heart. He is the Good Shepherd. Loving the sheep is his style.

This brings us to the next principle drawn from the leadership style of Jesus:

Principle 3

Good shepherds know their sheep.
Good leaders know their followers.

4 Man's Rules Versus God's Principles

Before founding The Church of The Apostles, I was managing director for the Haggai Institute. During that time, I spoke to a group of lay leaders at a large church that was struggling with a personnel issue, and some of the lay leaders asked for my advice.

A woman on the church support staff was approaching her sixty-fifth birthday, and the church had a mandatory retirement age of sixty-five. This woman, however, enjoyed excellent health and, because of a mix-up regarding her Social Security status, she faced the prospect of having no income for the coming year. So she asked if she could continue working.

After explaining the situation to me, the head of the personnel committee said, "I felt terrible saying no to her, but we have a mandatory retirement-age policy, and we can't break the rules."

"But isn't she an excellent worker?" I said.

"Oh, absolutely. One of the best workers we've ever had."

"And doesn't she hold a very responsible position?"

"That's true. In fact, she does the work of at least two people, and she really keeps things running smoothly."

"And isn't it true that you currently have no one to replace her?"

"That's also true."

"So if you force her to retire right now, it's going to cause hardship on her and a major disruption in the functioning of the church staff."

"Yes, unfortunately."

"Then why are you forcing this woman to retire when she can still do her job well and the church still needs her?"

"Well," he said, "we really have no choice. The policy is quite clear." He opened the church policy manual to the appropriate page and showed it to me. "See?"

"Yes, I see. But who set that policy?"

"I don't know. I suppose the policy was set by a personnel committee in the past. They were trying to look ahead and anticipate problems, and they made rules for us to follow."

"Don't you see?" I said. "The policy itself is creating the problem. It's creating a serious problem for this employee. And it's creating a serious problem for the church. The policy helps no one, and it disrupts everything."

"But what else can we do? The policy clearly states—"

And no matter how much I tried to reason with him, he wouldn't budge. He wouldn't consider amending the policy or making an exception to the policy. It was as if the personnel policy were carved in stone, like the Ten Commandments.

This is the mindset of legalism, and this mindset has oppressed the human race since the dawn of civilization.

Jesus Versus Man-Made Regulations

Jesus once encountered a man with a crippling illness. This man, who had been disabled for thirty-eight years, lay by a pool called Bethesda. Many other sick people were around that pool because they believed that at certain times an angel came and stirred the waters. According to legend, the first person into the water would receive a miracle of healing.

Jesus went to the disabled man and said, "Do you want to be healed?"

The man responded at first with an excuse: "Sir, I have no one to put me into the pool when the water is stirred up, and while I am going another steps down before me."

But Jesus ignored the man's excuse and said, "Get up, take up your bed, and walk." And at once, the man got to his feet, picked up his bed, and began to walk.

But that was not the end of the story. As recounted in John 5, the story contains this significant detail: "Now that day was the Sabbath."

When the religious leaders, the opponents of Jesus, saw the healed man walking and carrying his bed, they angrily confronted him, saying, "It is the Sabbath, and it is not lawful for you to take up your bed."

Now, you might think these religious leaders would be happy to learn that the man had been delivered from thirty-eight years as a hopeless invalid. But they were not happy. In fact, they were *enraged* because Jesus had healed the man on the Sabbath. There were rules and regulations about doing work on the Sabbath, and they would rather see the rules and regulations followed to the letter than see a sick man receive God's mercy on the holy day.

If you think about it for a moment, you quickly see the absurdity of the religious leaders' position. After all, a miracle of healing was proof of the messiahship of Jesus. Where did Jesus acquire the power to heal? From God. So how could Jesus be breaking God's law and offending God's will if God himself gave Jesus the power to heal?

But the opponents of Jesus didn't examine the evidence. They didn't consider the matter rationally. They were so blinded by their hatred of Jesus that they couldn't think straight.

It's true, of course, that God, through Moses, had given a commandment about the Sabbath: "Remember the Sabbath day, to keep it holy. Six days you shall labor, and do all your work, but the seventh day is a Sabbath to the LORD your God" (Exodus 20:8-10). But over the years, the religious leaders had added hundreds of man-made laws to God's simple command, and these legalistic requirements had kept the Jewish people oppressed.

So the religious leaders confronted the man as he carried his bed and demanded to know who had healed him. The man couldn't tell them because he didn't know who Jesus was. Later, after the man encountered Jesus in the temple, he went and told the religious leaders who had healed him. When they went and confronted Jesus, he told them he was doing the work of his Father—and they became even *more* enraged because by calling God his Father, Jesus was making himself equal with God.

This story illustrates one of the most important aspects of the leadership style of Jesus: He was willing to break with custom and tradition and man-made rules in order to meet desperate needs. If a man needed healing, Jesus didn't consult the Pharisees' rule books to see if healing were allowed on that particular day. He put compassion and mercy ahead of rules and regulations.

Someone once said, "The religious leaders loved things and used people, but Jesus loved people and used things." That's an apt summation of the difference between Jesus and his opponents. The point of the story is not that we should look for any excuse to break regulations or violate the rules. Jesus didn't violate the rules simply to be rebellious. Instead, he was illustrating that people come ahead of rules and regulations. Jesus put compassion ahead of legalism.

Institutions and Regulations

During my graduate studies, I researched institutions and social movements and learned that the founders of any institution, whether religious or secular, almost invariably criticize other, more established institutions. For example, a new company will compensate for its small size by criticizing the bigness of other companies: "The guys in those big, impersonal companies treat you like a number, but we give you *personal* service."

When a new congregation or denomination is formed, the members often feel disenchanted with the group they just left. They see the previous body as having become too large, impersonal, institutional, and uncaring. They criticize the old organization for rigidly observing rules and regulations and for caring only about programs, not people.

So the new organization sets out with vibrancy and an energetic sense of purpose. But in time, the new organization becomes an old and established organization. It becomes large and impersonal and increasingly bound by bureaucratic rules and regulations. In time, a radical, enthusiastic young leader arises, full of entrepreneurial spirit. He leads a rebellion against the silly old rules of the establishment and proclaims a new organization that is more people-oriented.

And the cycle begins all over again.

Similarly, when God communicated his Law to Moses, he handed down regulations that were for the good of the community. God didn't simply impose rules for the sake of perpetuating legalism. The Law of Moses was intended to protect, preserve, and instruct God's chosen people, Israel. Over time, however, the rational and compassionate Law of God was reinterpreted into an irrational and oppressive maze of regulations.

Ultimately, every Orthodox Jew in Israel had to observe 613 daily obligations. The teachers and interpreters of these laws divided them into two categories, 248 weighty obligations and 365 light precepts. Breaking the weighty rules was punished more severely than breaking the light rules, but all were rigidly enforced.

The leadership style of the scribes, Pharisees, and priests was one of burdening and oppressing the people. They derived their authority from ancient writings and precedents. When speaking on a given subject, they would cite an ancient teacher: "As Rabbi Hillel taught…"

Jesus came with a completely new and different leadership style. His teaching was rational and compassionate. He taught the people how to have better relationships, how to love and forgive each other, how to resolve conflicts, how to deal with worry and anxiety, and so forth. Unlike the nitpicky and irrational rule-making of the scribes and Pharisees, the teachings of Jesus made logical sense. His teachings were compassionate and liberating.

When Jesus spoke, he didn't derive his authority from other human teachers. In the Sermon on the Mount (Matthew 5–7), Jesus says again and again, "You have heard that it was said…But I say to you…" Instead of drawing authority from the teachers of the past, Jesus actually *contrasts* his teaching against the teachings of the past.

Jesus did not contradict the commandments of God or the Law of Moses. Instead, he showed how centuries of legalism had grown up around God's Law like a hedge of thorns, suppressing the truth and beauty of God's commandments. By healing the lame man on the Sabbath, Jesus showed how the religious leaders had turned man-made rules into idols that hid the truth of God's Law from their eyes.

In first-century Israel, the leading scholars debated endlessly the question, "Which commandment is the most important of all?" When the religious leaders tried to trick Jesus with that question, he replied, "The most important is, 'Hear, O Israel: The Lord our God, the Lord is one. And you shall love the Lord your God with all your heart and with all your soul and with all your mind and with all your strength.' The second is this: 'You shall love your neighbor as yourself.' There is no other commandment greater than these" (see Mark 12:28-34).

Jesus had a "back to basics" leadership style. He knew God's laws were meant to help people live fulfilled and purposeful lives, not hinder them and oppress them. So he put the emphasis back where it belongs—on compassion, love, faithfulness to others, and obedience to God. Instead of focusing on outward rituals and rules, Jesus focused on the inward reality of the heart.

Putting Human Needs Ahead of Human Customs

We shake our heads at the foolish legalism of the scribes and Pharisees. But as leaders we'd better be sure we're not guilty of the same fallacies and errors they committed. We'd better be sure that all the rules we observe are truly God's commandments. Otherwise we are guilty of inflicting man-made legalism on ourselves and our fellow Christians.

(Mind you, I have certain principles in place for me and my team. These guidelines are designed to protect us from both temptations and false accusations. So these rules serve to safeguard our character and reputations, not to confine or oppress us.)

Many well-intentioned missionaries in the nineteenth and twentieth centuries went to Africa and Asia seeking to evangelize those cultures for Christ. Unfortunately, some of them could not separate the Christian gospel from their Western culture. When they planted churches in those countries, the missionaries often imported Western art, music, and architecture. They built churches that would have been better suited for Boston or London than for a village in the Third World. They told these new Christians that their indigenous forms of music were heathen, and that they needed to sing the sacred music of Isaac Watts and Charles Wesley—music that was completely alien and incomprehensible to them.

I wonder if Jesus might have said to these well-intentioned missionaries, "You care more about your musical tastes and architectural forms than you do about the needs of these people. But I say to you, let them rejoice. Let them worship in their own words, in their own style of music."

The leadership style of Jesus puts people first, man-made rules second. A Christlike leader must be willing to change customs, modify traditions, and turn sacred cows into hamburger for the sake of the authentic and true needs of people.

This is not to say that tradition is without value. Some traditions are very important, and we shouldn't shatter tradition simply to be trendy and cool. But we should continually evaluate our rules, regulations, customs, and traditions, making sure they are truly biblical and they continue to serve a positive function in our lives. If manmade laws and traditions interfere with meeting the desperate needs of people, then it's time to rewrite them.

This brings us to our next leadership principle:

Principle 4

Authentic leaders place human needs
ahead of human customs.

This principle is easier to state than it is to apply. It can be difficult to distinguish a worn-out tradition from a timeless truth. We become attached to old-fashioned rules and regulations, and we fail to recognize the creative activity of the Holy Spirit.

If we don't want to end up resisting the Lord Jesus as the scribes and Pharisees did, then we need to ask ourselves: *Do I love God with all my heart? Do I truly love people and want what's best for them? Am I willing to be an agent for good change to do what God wants to do in my life? Or am I mired in hidebound legalism and inflexible traditionalism?*

There is no better way to show our love for God than to treat other people with love, grace, and kindness. A genuine leader demonstrates love for others by adapting human traditions to meet human needs.

5   Courage

Muhammad's followers today number over one billion people, or over 20 percent of the world's population. Islam, the religion he founded, is one of the fastest growing religions on earth.

Yet, at the beginning, Muhammad won very few converts to his new religion. Almost no one understood his message. He spoke of the blessedness of finding even one soul who would believe in him and his message. He even promised multiplied blessings on those first few converts for following him.

Down through the centuries, there have been many leaders, both religious and secular, who seemed willing to bribe others if they would become converts and followers. By "bribe," I mean to offer inducements, such as the promise of blessings or favors or a feeling that one has special insight and enlightenment. Many religious movements, businesses, and even entire nations have been started in this way. Leaders work hard to get the first few converts. Then, through the enthusiasm of those early converts, the leaders hope to build the kind of enthusiasm to grow the movement exponentially.

The gospels record the simple recruiting message of Jesus: "Follow me" (John 1:43). He made no great promises to his followers. In fact, he often emphasized the cost and the difficulty of being his disciple. He said that his followers had to bear their own cross and count the cost of discipleship, adding, "So therefore, any one of you who does not renounce all that he has cannot be my disciple" (Luke 14:33).

Even more surprising, Jesus did not cultivate friendships with influential people who could help him promote his cause. Instead, Jesus actually treated members of the influential class with a bluntness that bordered on harshness. John records a time when Nicodemus came to visit Jesus by night. He was a Pharisee, a member of the Jewish hierarchy, a representative of the religious order whose name means "the separated ones." The Pharisees considered themselves vastly more spiritual than ordinary people—and the Jewish people feared their power and influence.

Imagine how flattering it would have been if Nicodemus had become an early convert to the cause of Jesus. The Lord could have boasted, "I have disciples in high places." Yet Jesus did not go out of his way to recruit Nicodemus. He offered this Pharisee no greater welcome than he did anyone else. He made no promises, offered no inducements, and spoke no word of praise or flattery.

Instead, Jesus listened to the smooth words of Nicodemus: "Rabbi, we know that you are a teacher come from God, for no one can do these signs that you do unless God is with him" (John 3:2).

Jesus did not say, "Thank you for those kind words." He did not acknowledge the flattery of Nicodemus at all. Instead, he countered with a shocking and baffling message: "Truly, truly, I say to you, unless one is born again he cannot see the kingdom of God" (John 3:3).

This phrase "born again" is familiar in evangelical circles today. But when Jesus spoke those words to Nicodemus, they had a jarring effect. Born again? How could anyone be born a second time? These were not words that Nicodemus wanted to hear. In fact, Nicodemus scarcely understood them. No doubt, this proud Pharisee expected Jesus to be grateful for his unctuous words. Instead, Jesus replied with a riddle: "You must be born again" (John 3:7).

Apparently, Jesus had never read *How to Win Friends and Influence People*. Dale Carnegie could have told Jesus that he was violating the rules of good salesmanship by confronting Nicodemus with a baffling spiritual requirement. And Jesus would have replied, "But I'm not selling anything. I'm preaching the truth: You must be born again."

No Compromise

By the standards of modern salesmanship, Jesus made one of the worst mistakes possible in his late-night talk with Nicodemus. Every sales course I've ever heard of advises salespeople to immediately get on the good side of the prospective buyer. Salespeople are taught to use flattery and compliments, to be friendly and likable, and to keep smiling. Above all, a salesperson must avoid taking controversial positions and must keep the mood light and congenial. If you have strong convictions, keep them to yourself. Jesus broke all these rules.

Nicodemus, by contrast, seemed well-schooled in the techniques of salesmanship. He approached Jesus with patronizing flattery. Many people, eager to be accepted by the social elites, would have been seduced by the flattery of this Pharisee. You or I might have thought, *This man is saying such nice things about me! I certainly wouldn't want to say anything to offend him. Maybe I should tone down my rhetoric and stay on his good side.*

But Jesus would not water down his message. He stated his message boldly and forcefully, without compromise, whether he was speaking to the lowest outcast of society or a member of the Pharisee elite. Jesus was no respecter of persons. By speaking to Nicodemus as he did, Jesus showed courage bordering on audacity.

Jesus was no salesman (that is not to put down good and diligent salesmen). Rather, he was the very epitome of authentic leadership. So Jesus had a blunt, candid, yet patient intellectual encounter with Nicodemus the Pharisee. He cared enough about Nicodemus and his eternal fate to speak the uncompromised truth.

I once watched a televised conversation between a well-known Christian leader and an avowed humanist. It saddened me to see the Christian leader try to win the acceptance of the audience by watering down the claims of Jesus Christ. The more the audience heckled him, the more he compromised the gospel.

As leaders, we need to accept that we will often be called upon to defend unpopular positions—and we had better have the courage to defend our views boldly and without compromise, or we will cease to be leaders. Authentic leadership is marked by boldness, courage, and conviction. This is true whether one is leading in the religious realm or the secular world.

When we take a courageous stand, we are Christlike in character, integrity, and values. We must take a bold stand for our moral principles. Sure, it will sometimes cost us. We may be attacked face-to-face or in the media. But if you lack the courage and boldness to stand for your principles, then you shouldn't be in leadership.

Jesus didn't treat the gospel as a product to be packaged and sold. Jesus the Messiah never made an exaggerated sales pitch, never watered down the truth, and never compromised his unconditional love. He always spoke the truth in love.

A Courageous Stand for Integrity

My friend Barbara spent twenty years working as a reservation agent for a major airline. She did her job efficiently and courteously, but she got in trouble with her supervisors because of an overabundance of integrity. Her bosses told her she was putting her job at risk by being too honest.

What did Barbara do wrong? She gave customers accurate, complete information about service and price. If a prospective customer needed to fly at a particular time, and her airline did not have a flight scheduled at that time, she would provide information on flights with a rival airline.

Barbara understood that her job was to book flights and make money for her airline, but she also understood that her job involved customer satisfaction. Several times, her bosses reprimanded her for sending customers to the competition. But she courageously persisted in doing what she believed was right. Eventually, her bosses discovered that Barbara's integrity was actually making money for the airline.

Customers, impressed by Barbara's helpfulness and refreshing honesty, wrote letters thanking the airline for the actions of this one reservation agent. One customer wrote, "I travel a lot and I have never had anyone suggest another airline unless I insisted. She volunteered the information. I want you to know that from now on, you are my exclusive airline."

That company would have been wise to turn Barbara's example into a company policy. Unfortunately, they never encouraged other employees to follow Barbara's lead. But they did allow her to do her job as she saw fit, because it clearly paid off.

Whether there is a benefit to honesty and integrity, authentic leaders need to take a stand for the truth and for their values. As one leader said, "If I compromise on one principle with one customer, where do I draw the line?"

There is no one verse of Scripture where Jesus tells his followers to be courageous and stand firm for their values and principles. He never had to issue such a command. His example said it all.

In John 2, the greatest leader that ever lived stood boldly against the religious leaders of his day because they had turned God's house into a flea market. He braided a whip, strode through the temple courtyard, lashed at the money changers and merchants with the whip, and overturned their tables. As he did so, he rebuked them for their wicked practices.

A number of years ago, I was teaching on this passage in an adult Sunday school class. A young, successful businessman in the class said, "I've always thought that it was really dumb and pointless to clear the temple. After all, the very next day, the merchants set up their tables again and were back in business."

Before I could reply, a homemaker in the class responded, "Sometimes we have to choose symbolic action. Jesus couldn't clean out the temple every day. He didn't intend to do that. Instead, he used that action as a platform to send a message to the entire Jewish nation. By one significant act, he showed the people what is right and what is wrong."

I couldn't have come up with a better answer. We need more people today who will do the right thing, say the right thing, and send a message to our culture, even if it seems to make no practical difference. We need leaders who will courageously speak the truth in love to our generation.

God did not send us out into the world to be successful. He sent us out to be faithful and to speak his truth. And what is success anyway? If we obey biblical principles, we can leave the results to him. We need to imitate Christ's courage to confront sin, evil, and injustice in our society. Whether the world responds to our message is not up to us. The results belong to God.

Courage for the Battle

The leadership arena is a battlefield. It takes courage to step onto the battlefield and fight for what is right. Courage is not a lack of fear. Even courageous people tremble at times. But courageous people accept the risk, feel the fear, and do what is right anyway. As the easily frightened Piglet once said to his friend Winnie-the-Pooh, "I didn't mean to be brave. It just happened when I panicked."

A leader may seem confident on the outside, but that doesn't mean there are no butterflies on the inside. Leaders often have moments of self-doubt when they privately pray, *Lord, am I doing the right thing?*

Sometimes doing the right thing doesn't *seem* right. Sometimes doing the right thing feels terrible. When we have to reprimand a subordinate, discipline a child, or confront someone we care about over a sin or scandal, we feel miserable. We know it's the right thing to do, but we wish we didn't have to do it. Leaders are often called to perform unpleasant tasks. That's why leadership takes courage.

Martin Luther, the fiery reformer of the sixteenth century, was a leader of courage. He defied the institutional church, the pope, and other religious and secular officials. In 1521, he was summoned to appear before the Diet (assembly) of the city of Worms in Germany. Though he was promised safe escort, Luther knew that he risked his life by appearing before the Diet. More than a hundred years earlier, the Czech reformer John Hus had been promised safe escort to the Council of Konstanz, yet his opponents imprisoned him, and then burned him at the stake.

Church officials promised Martin Luther that he would be forgiven if he would repent of his "errors" and return to "the true faith." Luther knew this promise was meaningless, since church officials considered promises to "heretics" nonbinding. He also knew that thousands of Christians had been tortured to death by the corrupt institutional church during the infamous Spanish Inquisition.

Luther arrived in the city of Worms, but the court allowed him no opportunity to defend his beliefs. Instead, he was presented with a list of his "errors." Luther knew that the court could decide whether he lived or died. Nevertheless, Luther told the court:

> Unless I am convicted of error by the testimony of Scripture or…by manifest reasoning I stand convicted by the Scriptures to which I have appealed, and my conscience is taken captive by God's Word, I cannot and will not recant anything, for to act against our conscience is neither safe for us, nor open to us. On this I take my stand. I can do no other. God help me. Amen.[1]

Down through the centuries, God has appointed leaders to make a courageous stand for truth, righteousness, and integrity. He has worked through people who, even though their knees were knocking and their voices shaking, had the courage to answer his call and step onto the battlefield. Again and again, Christian leaders have stepped forward and altered the course of history.

You and I must be prepared to answer that same call.

Courage Goes to Work

Some years ago, a Christian man in Australia—we'll call him Jim—took a job with the government. He had been in the job for only a week when his superior said, "Jim, would you like to earn some overtime?"

"I sure would," he said.

His first evening on the overtime shift, Jim watched as his boss and his fellow employees sat at a table and played cards. Baffled, Jim said, "What about the work we're supposed to do?"

His supervisor said, "What work? 'Overtime' means we stay late, play cards, punch our time cards, and collect extra pay. Sit down. We'll deal you in."

"If we're going to be paid to work," Jim said, "then let's work. Otherwise you're just cheating the taxpayers."

From then on, Jim's boss and coworkers treated him as an outsider. They gave him all the worst jobs that no one else wanted. They called him "Bible basher" and "Jesus freak."

Jim refused to compromise his faith and values. After a while, his supervisor tried to break down Jim's integrity. "Look," he said, "you're a nice guy, trying to do the right thing. But all it's getting you is trouble. If you'd stop being such a fanatic and start going along and getting along, people would get off your back. Plus, you'd make a lot more money."

"I only want to get paid for doing honest work," Jim replied. "You can't pay me enough to get me to compromise my Christian convictions."

The persecution and name-calling got worse and worse until Jim finally had to leave. Before he left, the head of the department called Jim into his office and said, "I want you to know that your courageous stand for your principles has not gone unnoticed. There are people at the highest level of this agency who are talking about how conscientious you are."

Jim's courage had made him a leader—and God honored Jim for his courageous stand. God has promised that he will honor those who honor him with the way they live their lives (see 1 Samuel 2:30).

This doesn't mean God will always reward you in a material way. In fact, there is often a price to be paid for courage. Your courageous and principled stand may cost you your career, your income, your reputation, your friendships, and more. An authentic leader is willing to pay the price to maintain his integrity. Pleasing God comes first, ahead of pleasing oneself.

The apostle Paul struggled with the question of whether he should please God or seek the approval of others. He speaks to this dilemma in the book of Galatians. He had taught the Galatians the gospel message that God saves by grace through faith in Jesus Christ and nothing more. After Paul left the region of Galatia, a group of false teachers (called Judaizers) moved in and told the Galatian Christians that they needed to practice the ceremonial law of Judaism, especially circumcision, in addition to believing in Jesus.

"I am astonished," Paul wrote, "that you are so quickly deserting him who called you in the grace of Christ and are turning to a different gospel" (Galatians 1:6). Paul pleaded with the Galatian believers to reject the false gospel of the Judaizers, adding, "For am I now seeking the approval of man, or of God? Or am I trying to please man? If I were still trying to please man, I would not be a servant of Christ" (Galatians 1:10).

It took courage for Paul to write those words. His message was confrontational and controversial. It angered many in the Galatian church. Paul probably lost friends over that debate, but he refused to compromise the gospel for the sake of his popularity.

Nicodemus: The Rest of the Story

After the first appearance of Nicodemus the Pharisee in John 3, where he visits Jesus by night, we encounter him again in John 7. There, the religious leaders gather to condemn Jesus without trial. Nicodemus speaks up and says, "Does our law judge a man without first giving him a hearing and learning what he does?" (John 7:51).

The religious leaders sneer at Nicodemus and insult him, saying, "Are you from Galilee too? Search and see that no prophet arises from Galilee" (John 7:52).

Later, after the crucifixion of Jesus, Nicodemus goes with Joseph of Arimathea, the wealthy nobleman whose tomb Jesus would be buried in. Joseph and Nicodemus bring a hundred pounds of burial spices to prepare the body of Jesus. By doing so, Nicodemus openly declares himself to be a disciple of Jesus.

It took considerable courage for Nicodemus to publicly identify himself as a follower of Jesus of Nazareth. There was a very real possibility that the religious leaders, having crucified Jesus, might come after his followers next. Perhaps the moment of Nicodemus's conversion came during the crucifixion itself. It may well be that Nicodemus stood at the foot of the cross, watching Jesus die, and remembering how Jesus had said to him during his late-night visit, "And as Moses lifted up the serpent in the wilderness, so must the Son of Man be lifted up, that whoever believes in him may have eternal life" (John 3:14-15).

Nicodemus was transformed—and his transformation began the night Jesus showed courageous leadership in dealing with Nicodemus and his questions. Courage is a crucial dimension of the leadership style of Jesus.

This brings us to the next leadership principle that emerges from the life of Jesus:

Principle 5

In my servant leadership,
I can have courage for every leadership battle.

6   Gentleness

I am always astounded at the way Jesus spoke to people. The communication style of Jesus was perfectly balanced. He was assertive yet never pushy. He was gentle but never timid. He confronted people (such as the Samaritan woman at the well) without condemning them.

When his enemies tried to corner him, he adroitly eluded their traps and turned the tables on them, putting his adversaries on the defensive. In Luke's gospel, for example, the religious leaders challenged the authority of Jesus to teach and preach in the Jerusalem temple. "Tell us by what authority you do these things," they demanded, "or who it is that gave you this authority."

Jesus replied, "I also will ask you a question. Now tell me, was the baptism of John from heaven or from man?"

It was a masterful response, like making a move on a chessboard and announcing, "Check!" The religious leaders were so perplexed that they had to step aside and discuss their answer among themselves. They whispered, "If we say, 'From heaven,' he will say, 'Why did you not believe him?' But if we say, 'From man,' all the people will stone us to death, for they are convinced that John was a prophet."

Finally, they turned to Jesus, shrugged, and said, "We do not know."

And Jesus replied, "Neither will I tell you by what authority I do these things" (see Luke 20:1-8).

Jesus corrected his disciples when they needed it—yet his rebukes were more gentle and loving than the kindest affirmations of most people. On the night he was betrayed, he was in the upper room with the Twelve. To demonstrate the kind of servanthood he wanted his disciples to practice, he took a basin of water and a towel, and he began to wash the disciples' feet.

Seeing what Jesus was doing, Peter proudly refused. "You shall never wash my feet," he said. Jesus answered firmly yet gently, "If I do not wash you, you have no share with me" (see John 13:1-15).

As C.S. Lewis wrote in his autobiography, "The hardness of God is kinder than the softness of men, and His compulsion is our liberation."[1] Throughout the four gospels, we see evidence after evidence that this statement is true. One of the key qualities of the leadership style of Jesus is gentleness.

Meekness Is Not Weakness

Nowhere is the gentleness of Jesus displayed more clearly than in the story of the woman caught in adultery. Early in the morning, he was in the temple court, teaching the people. As he was teaching, some scribes and Pharisees approached him, dragging a woman along. They interrupted Jesus and shoved the woman forward, saying, "Teacher, this woman has been caught in the act of adultery. Now in the Law, Moses commanded us to stone such women. So what do you say?"

It was yet another attempt by the religious leaders to trap Jesus, but as they attacked him, he almost seemed to ignore them. He bent down and wrote with his finger in the dust—and I would love to know what he wrote! Finally, he looked up at his adversaries and said, "Let him who is without sin among you be the first to throw a stone at her." Then he went back to writing with his finger in the dust.

One by one, the religious leaders drifted away, silenced and shamed by the Lord's response. When they had gone, Jesus said, "Woman, where are they? Has no one condemned you?" She replied that no one remained. "Neither do I condemn you," Jesus said. "Go, and from now on sin no more" (John 8:1-11). Jesus did not excuse or condone her sin, nor did he condemn her and lecture her. Instead, he did two things:

First, Jesus accepted her. It was clear from his words that Jesus was aware of this woman's sin. But he did not increase the burden of guilt she already felt. Instead, he released her from condemnation. He accepted her.

Most of us have enough guilt weighing us down without other people stacking additional guilt on top of us. When we fail, we usually know it. Our sense of sin, shame, and failure often makes us feel unworthy.

When the religious leaders dragged the woman before Jesus, she wasn't the only sinner there. The religious leaders were sinners as well—arrogant, prideful, self-righteous hypocrites, every one of them. But they hid their sin even from themselves until Jesus forced them to examine themselves.

Second, Jesus forgave her. "Neither do I condemn you," he said. "Go, and from now on sin no more." I marvel at that statement. It's so simple, so direct. Jesus said everything the woman needed to hear in those few words. He let her know she was forgiven, yet he also commanded her to leave her life of sin. She needed no lectures. She needed forgiveness. And that is what Jesus gave her, freely and graciously.

Jesus embodied grace as well as truth, and the grace of Jesus was expressed as gentleness. Tough, assertive leaders are often drawn to the toughness and assertiveness of Jesus in his battles with the Pharisees, his cleansing of the temple, and his condemnation of oppression and hypocrisy. But we must never forget the gentleness of Jesus. In all of his interactions with people, he struck the perfect balance of afflicting the comfortable and comforting the afflicted. Though he fiercely confronted religious hypocrisy and spiritual abuse, he was compassionate and gentle toward those who suffered from guilt, grief, sorrow, and shame.

The gospel of Mark captures the gentle and compassionate spirit of Jesus in this account: "When he went ashore he saw a great crowd, and he had compassion on them, because they were like sheep without a shepherd. And he began to teach them many things" (Mark 6:34).

In our culture, we tend to think of gentleness (and related qualities like humility and meekness) as *weakness*. Yet these qualities may, in fact, indicate a far greater strength of character and personality than the so-called strength that prompts us to bark orders.

The apostle Paul lists gentleness as one of the fruit of the Spirit (see Galatians 5:22-23). I used to wonder why Paul seemed to prize gentleness so much. My impression of Paul was that he was often feisty and combative, straight to the point, and quick to set people straight. But I have since come to understand that it is possible to be both assertive and gentle at the same time. That is undoubtedly part of what John meant when he said that Jesus is full of both grace and truth. We tend to err toward being either all truth (being blunt and rudely confrontational) or all grace (being so mild and wimpy that we compromise the truth).

Jesus is the epitome of grace and truth in perfect balance.

The Three Ingredients of Gentleness

The leadership quality of gentleness consists of three parts or ingredients.

The first part is *kindness* or *consideration*. An authentically gentle leader demonstrates consideration for the feelings of others. He or she would never intentionally hurt, belittle, shame, or embarrass another person.

The second part is *submission*. In the biblical sense, this refers to submission to the will of God, a willing obedience to God's Word and God's leading. Another word for submission is *meekness*.

The Bible describes Moses as "very meek, more than all people who were on the face of the earth" (Numbers 12:3). Yet, as we read through the story of Moses, we see a man who was bold and out-spoken, a leader of the Hebrew people, a man who dared to confront the Pharaoh of Egypt face-to-face. Moses, the meekest man on the face of the earth, took a bold and courageous stand for the truth. Meekness does not mean timidity or shyness; it means power under control.

Jesus also displayed this same quality of meekness. He submitted to the will of God the Father, going willingly and obediently to the cross when he could have taken an easier way out. It isn't possible for us to fully appreciate what the meekness and obedience of Jesus cost him. But we know that the act of submission was so excruciatingly difficult that Jesus sweat drops of blood as he prayed in the Garden of Gethsemane. The amazing meekness and strength of Jesus enabled him to pray, "Father, if you are willing, remove this cup from me. Nevertheless, not my will, but yours, be done" (Luke 22:42).

The third part of gentleness is *a teachable spirit*, a willingness to learn and to be corrected. A truly gentle person readily admits that he or she does not have all the answers, and is always open to new ideas and new depths of understanding. The Italian painter Titian (1488–1576), who was famed for paintings of mythological and religious subjects, was still painting when he was well into his eighties. Once, after completing one of his masterworks very late in his life, he put down his brush and palette, then said to his assistant (in all sincerity), "I think I am beginning to learn something about painting." That is a teachable spirit—a spirit of authentic gentleness.

From a worldly perspective, words like *gentleness* and *meekness* convey a sense of weakness. But from a Christian perspective, gentleness and meekness actually mean "strength under control." A gentle leader is smart but feels no need to prove it, strong but feels no need to demonstrate it, confident but feels no need to tear others down. The gentle leader is strong, but keeps his or her strength under control.

Strong Enough to Be Gentle

A friend of mine was raised in a poor family. His parents could afford to give him the barest of necessities and little more. He was a bright young man with an inquisitive mind and he loved to read. He went regularly to a pharmacy where he would hide in a corner and read the magazines, especially the comic books. He treated the magazines with care so that no one would complain about damaged pages.

One day he went beyond just reading the magazines. He slipped one inside his shirt and walked out the door. Having gotten away with one theft, he went on to stealing more and more magazines. Soon, stealing had become a habit.

Eventually, the pharmacist caught him and made him take the magazines out of his shirt. Terrified, my friend wondered what the pharmacist would do about it. Would he call the police? Would he call his parents?

The pharmacist sat my friend down and told him it was wrong to take property that didn't belong to him, and if he continued stealing, he'd end up in serious trouble. Then the pharmacist did something amazing. He put his hand on my friend's shoulder and said, "Please don't do that again."

My friend later told me, "I never did it again, and I never forgot that man. He would have been within his rights to call the police. Instead, he treated me kindly, and I didn't want to let him down."

It takes great strength to be gentle, as the pharmacist was toward my friend. Not every leader knows how to demonstrate gentleness. Many leaders look down on those who are gentle, thinking they are weak, ineffective, or even stupid.

But Jesus showed us that gentleness is strength. The practice of gentleness may seem to be a lost art in many of our business dealings, our classrooms, our homes, and even our churches. But it is an art that every authentic leader should master. Gentleness is an essential dimension of the leadership style of Jesus.

That's why the next leadership principle that emerges from the life of Jesus is:

Principle 6

Only the leader who is truly strong
can be truly gentle.

7   Generosity

A businessman noticed a promising young man named Timothy who attended his church. When Timothy's parents died, he had to drop out of college and work to support his two younger brothers. After praying for guidance, the businessman felt led to make Timothy an offer: "I'll lend you all the money you need to stay in college, and I'll give your younger brothers part-time jobs."

Timothy was overwhelmed by the man's generosity. He returned to school, completed his education, and even got a master's degree. Five years after the businessman made this generous offer, Timothy had a well-paying job and a secure future. By this time, his younger brothers were also doing well in college.

Timothy went to his benefactor and said, "I'm ready to start paying you back. I can begin by making payments of two hundred dollars a month, if that's all right."

"No," the businessman replied, "when I lent you that money, I had a different plan in mind. I don't want you to pay me back. Instead, I want you to keep an eye out for some young person who is as deserving as you were. I want you to do the same thing for that person that I did for you."

This businessman was a leader who practiced the leadership style of Jesus. He exemplified the leadership trait of generosity.

The Generosity of Jesus

We see the generosity of Jesus demonstrated in his feeding of the five thousand—the only miracle of Jesus that is recorded in all four gospels. Clearly, this event made a deep impression on the gospel writers and the early church.

Jesus took one boy's lunch and multiplied it so there was enough food to feed everyone present. The accounts say there were five thousand *men* present, which means there might have been an equal number of women and children present.

Jesus could have warned the crowd in the morning that they should bring a sack lunch. He could have shrugged off the needs of those people as "not my problem." The disciples knew that the people would be hungry, and they offered a sensible suggestion to Jesus: Send everybody home before dark.

But Jesus didn't send the people away. He provided for them. That's the generosity of Jesus. He gave when he didn't have to and with no expectation of anything in return.

Jesus provided for the people what they could not provide for themselves. In this case it was food. On another occasion, when he encountered a blind man (John 9), he provided the gift of sight. At the wedding feast in Cana (John 2), Jesus provided wine.

There is a common image of leaders as people who are ruthlessly ambitious, and who will step on anyone to get what they want. It's true that many people have achieved power through greed and selfish ambition. Those people may be bosses, but they are not true leaders because no one admires them, no one sees them as a role model, and people of character don't want to be like them.

Leaders are role models, and they inspire imitation. I have known many people who are leaders in business, government, the church, education, and other fields of endeavor, and genuine leaders are always people who give generously. They don't just care about their image. They genuinely care about others and give of themselves so that others can succeed.

According to the business mentoring company Management Mentors, the generosity of top executives, as expressed through mentoring, is a key factor in successful careers and organizations:

- Fully 75 percent of executives list mentoring as a key factor in their career success.
- The productivity of managing executives increased 88 percent when mentoring was involved.
- 71 percent of Fortune 500 companies (that is, the most successful companies in the world) use mentoring as a key training tool.
- 77 percent of businesses say that mentoring programs increase employee retention. [1]

Clearly, the most successful leaders and companies are those that generously practice mentoring. They are thinking long term. They don't simply use people and then throw them away; they seek to build knowledge and character traits into people, help them along in their careers, and retain them over the long haul. These leaders and companies don't just think about profit; they are concerned about people. By caring for the people who work for them, they help themselves and their bottom line.

Sharing Time, Attention, and Experience

The late Cecil B. Day Sr. founded the Days Inn motel chain in 1970, and within eight years had a system of three hundred motels throughout North America. Mr. Day was a philanthropist and a committed Christian, as well as a successful hotelier. He placed copies of the Good News Bible New Testament in every room and encouraged his guests to take a free copy. The Days Inn franchise has since become part of the Wyndham Hotel Group, and today there are more than nineteen hundred Days Inn motels around the world.

Cecil Day was known as a man who worked hard to produce wealth so that he could donate money to causes that honored God. Before his death, he donated his entire estate to Christian causes and aided the work of many deserving evangelists, missionaries, and Christian workers. His life was devoted to generous giving.

Generosity takes many forms. It doesn't mean merely giving

money, but also giving time, compassion, and a listening ear. Leaders who live according to the leadership style of Jesus know that giving of oneself can often be more costly and just as effective as giving millions of dollars. Here are some of the ways that authentic leaders show Christlike generosity:

1. *They generously give their time.* Christlike leaders see themselves as servants not bosses. They don't hoard their time; they *invest* their time in others. Some of the most effective laypeople in the church come from a leadership background in the business world. One regional sales manager told me, "I give my employer my best. At the church, I use the best business practices I know in order to serve Jesus Christ." One of the ways he does this is by leading his church's evangelism program.

2. *They generously give their attention.* I recently heard about a CEO of a retirement community in the Midwest who underscores his open-door policy by locating his office near the front entrance of the facility and keeping not one but two doors open at all times. "He's the most accessible person in our organization," said one fellow executive. "He's never too busy to talk to any employee." An open door is a visual symbol, and leaders who are truly generous with their time use that symbol as a way of communicating authentic generosity of time and attention. An open door says, "I want to hear what you have to say, I want to help you solve your problems, I want you to know I will listen to you and care about your needs."

3. *They generously give of their experience.* The best leaders have learned many lessons in their leadership careers. When asked, they are willing and eager to share their experience with others. One of the most effective ways of sharing our experience is through mentoring relationships.

Mentoring is a personal relationship between an experienced, knowledgeable person and a less-experienced person, involving conversations, instruction, guidance, and challenge. Senior executives share their experience by mentoring younger executives; senior pastors mentor young pastors and seminarians; seasoned authors mentor young writers; adults mentor youth.

According to the National Mentoring Partnership, more than eighteen million young people need a mentor, but only three million are involved in mentoring relationships. Young people who are involved in mentoring relationships are far more likely to stay in school than those who aren't in a mentoring relationship. They are also 46 percent less likely to use drugs and 27 percent less likely to use alcohol than their nonmentored peers. [2]

Linda Taylor, president and CEO of Koach Konsulting, recalls, "My life is an example of the impact mentoring can have on the life of an at-risk child growing up in an inner city...I still remember the conversations [my mentor and I] had as she shared her experience and her story. More importantly, she shared what was possible for me and she encouraged me to value my education and to dream big, really big. Her presence in my life made a difference and is a major reason I am who I am." [3]

Great leaders who follow the leadership style of Jesus are generous with their resources, their time, their wisdom, and their insight. They give as Jesus gave, expecting nothing in return.

The Giving Principle

Jesus said, "You received without paying; give without pay" (see Matthew 10:8b). Or as the New International Version renders it, "Freely you have received; freely give." In God's economy, we never lose by giving. We only gain.

To worldly cynics, this may sound absurd, but as believers, we know it's true. Leaders give of themselves, and by giving they produce better relationships, better organizations, and a more satisfying life for themselves and others. By generously giving of ourselves daily, we turn the golden rule into a practical way of life.

Generosity is not a natural impulse. We learn to live generously by the example of others. Those who have been mentored, taught, befriended, or helped by a generous leader are more likely to live a lifestyle of generosity toward others.

Authentic generosity is not a role we play or an image we project. It must come from within, motivated by love, not by a desire to get something in return. The paradox of generosity is that when we give freely, without being repaid in any way, we truly receive. What do we receive? We receive the joy of giving, of serving, and of being approved by our Lord.

When I started the Anglican Church of The Apostles in Atlanta, the first six years we met at a private school. About one mile from that private school is a large, thriving Pentecostal church. This church was founded and pastored by one of God's most generous servant leaders, Paul Walker.

When I had the joy of meeting Dr. Walker, I told him that I had admired him for many years. He immediately offered any help he could give me. I said, "Paul, we're only a mile or two at the most away from you."

"We both work for the same Master," he said. "There are millions to be reached in Atlanta, and we can't do it all ourselves."

I thought, *That's generosity!* From that moment we began a special friendship, and I will always owe Dr. Walker a debt of gratitude for his frequent wise counsel and the generous gift of his time and experience.

Dr. Walker is living out the example of Jesus as recorded in Mark 9 and Luke 9. After Jesus had sent out the Twelve to preach and heal in his name, John came to him and said, "Teacher, we saw someone casting out demons in your name, and we tried to stop him, because he was not following us."

Jesus replied, "Do not stop him…for the one who is not against us is for us."

The Lord Jesus, our leadership role model, practiced true generosity in everything he did. Authentic leaders give generously, freely, expecting nothing in return—and are blessed and rewarded with joy. This brings us to our next leadership principle:

Principle 7

Authentic leaders give generously.

8   Truthfulness

It's a TV drama cliché, and I'm sure you've seen it many times before. The doctor runs a battery of tests on the patient, and then he takes off his stethoscope and sighs deeply. The patient's anguished wife asks, "Is he going to be all right, doctor?"

He looks at her, grim-faced. "Do you want the truth?" he asks.

At that point, what is she supposed to say? What would you say in that situation? "No, doctor, please lie to me. I can't deal with the truth. Just say something to make me feel good."

No one would say that. We may, at times, fear the truth. We may have trouble facing the truth. We especially fear the truth when the truth exposes our sins. Many of us are very skilled at hiding from the truth about ourselves. But no one wants to be lied to.

Leaders who deceive others or deceive themselves soon find themselves without followers and without a reason to lead. Leaders must face the truth and they must tell the truth, especially when the truth is unpleasant to hear.

Embodying the Truth

What is truth?

That is the question posed by a Roman governor two thousand years ago when he was tested by history. He had an opportunity to find the truth and act according to the truth. Instead, he failed the test.

The gospel of John tells the story of an amazing dialogue between

Jesus of Nazareth and the Roman governor of Judea, Pontius Pilate. Their conversation occurred when the corrupt religious leaders brought Jesus before Pilate to be judged and sentenced to death. The religious leaders had no power to impose capital punishment. Only the Roman government could do so. So the religious leaders went to Pilate and sought his complicity in their plot against Jesus. They accused Jesus of claiming to be a king and of being the ringleader of a rebellion against Caesar.

Pilate asked Jesus about their accusation, saying, "Are you the King of the Jews?"

Jesus replied, "You say that I am a king. For this purpose I was born and for this purpose I have come into the world—to bear witness to the truth. Everyone who is of the truth listens to my voice."

Pilate replied, "What is truth?" (see John 18:28-38).

The Roman governor was face-to-face with the truth, yet he didn't recognize it. For as Jesus himself had told Thomas a few hours earlier in the upper room, "I am the way, and the truth, and the life. No one comes to the Father except through me" (John 14:6).

Jesus embodies truth. He stands for truth. He will not deviate from the truth. There is no greater leadership example of truthfulness for us to follow than the example of Jesus. As John wrote in the first chapter of his gospel, "For the law was given through Moses; grace and truth came through Jesus Christ" (John 1:17).

As leaders who follow the leadership style of Jesus, we must face the truth, embody the truth, and tell the truth at all times. Being fallible, we don't know all the truth there is to know. But we owe it to our Lord, our followers, and the organizations we serve to always be leaders of integrity.

Our commitment to the truth must be absolute and unswerving. As the apostle Paul once wrote, "Finally, brothers, whatever is true, whatever is honorable, whatever is just, whatever is pure, whatever is lovely, whatever is commendable, if there is any excellence, if there is anything worthy of praise, think about these things" (Philippians 4:8).

Jesus was a leader who bore witness to the truth. His followers listened to his voice, and they knew the truth when they heard it. If we lead by the leadership style of Jesus, then we too will bear witness to the truth, and our followers will hear the truth whenever we speak.

Speaking the Truth

Many years ago, several friends and I went to hear a speaker give an address at a convention. I didn't know the man personally, but my friends did, and we planned to go out for coffee with him after his talk. As I sat and listened to his speech that evening, I was—to be candid—disappointed. His message didn't seem well-organized, and I had a hard time following it. In fact, it was difficult to keep my mind from wandering.

Afterward, my friends, the speaker, and I sat together in a coffee shop. We introduced ourselves to each other, and the speaker said, "What did you think of my message?"

I looked around at my companions, and I could see by their expressions that they had all been as disappointed as I was—but no one wanted to say so!

"You spoke with energy and sincerity tonight," one man said. "I can tell you really enjoy public speaking."

"I could tell you put a lot of preparation into that message," a second man added.

Finally, the speaker turned to me. I had to say something, but what? I didn't want to hurt the man's feelings, but I could hardly avoid being hurtful if I spoke the unvarnished truth. It was especially awkward being asked in front of other people.

After some hemming and hawing, I said, "I'd better pass. I just wasn't with it today. I couldn't keep my mind focused, so you'd better not ask me."

To this day, it bothers me that I gave that answer. It was not a truthful answer. Yes, he put me on the spot, and in hindsight I wish I had said something like, "Candidly, I did not like the message. If you're interested, I'd be happy to get together with you later and we could talk about it in detail."

I felt so bad about giving a less-than-truthful answer that I discussed my dilemma with a friend. After I explained what happened, my friend said, "If people don't want to hear the truth, they shouldn't ask for it. If someone asks for your opinion in front of other people, I think you have an obligation to give your honest opinion."

I think that's good advice. I suspect that the speaker was looking more for affirmation, even flattery, not the truth. But if you ask for someone's honest opinion, never be dismayed when they give it to you.

It is natural for most people to want to avoid unpleasantness, confrontation, or hurting people's feelings. It's a dilemma I have faced many times, and I have to admit that I have dealt with such situations with diplomatic half-truths far too many times. I'm not inclined to tell a bald-faced lie, but all too often, I end up speaking only part of the truth.

And when we speak less than the truth, we lie.

Mishandling the Truth

There are many ways to speak less than the truth, and we often don't realize it or even think about it. Some examples:

- We sing hymns of commitment to God, such as, "Take my life, and let it be consecrated, Lord, to Thee," yet we sing the words without meaning them, without even thinking about them. When we sing a hymn, we should either mean the words we sing, or we should be silent.

- We make promises that we have no intention of keeping. We say, "I'll pray for you," or "I'll call you next week," or

"I'll try to come," or "I'll keep it strictly confidential"—
and we know we won't.

- We remain silent when we should speak up, such as
  when an injustice is being committed. By our silence,
  we imply that we agree with what is taking place or
  being said.

- We say things to be polite, even though we don't mean
  them. For example, we tell people, "You must come for
  a visit," although we actually hope they won't.

- We inflate our résumés, crediting ourselves with exaggerated or false accomplishments, or we fail to correct the
  record when people give us credit we don't deserve.

We tend to think that such white lies are not *real* lies, but they
are. The world excuses little white lies, embellishments, exaggera-
tions, hyperbole, elaboration, and even whoppers. In fact, people in
the secular world think you are ridiculously puritanical and strait-
laced if you insist on maintaining absolute integrity.

Why do so many people today feel they must swear an oath in
order to be believed? We've all heard people say, "I swear on a stack
of Bibles, it's true!" Others even take the Lord's name in vain as they
swear an oath. People feel this is necessary because everyone lies so
casually, their unsworn word is simply not believable. And, in truth,
even their sworn word is worth very little.

The ancient Jews had a saying, "One who gives his word and
changes it is as evil as an idol worshiper." In other words, common
everyday speech was expected to be truthful; lying and promise-
breaking were considered sins of the first order, as repugnant as
idolatry. Taking an oath in that culture literally meant that God
was being invoked as a witness to the truthfulness of the speaker's
statement—and invoking God in that way was considered sinful,
because it meant that the speaker was taking the Lord's name in vain,
a violation of the Third Commandment (see Exodus 20:7).

The Third Commandment condemns making promises in the name of God that cannot or will not be fulfilled. In Numbers 30:2, God declares, "If a man vows a vow to the LORD, or swears an oath to bind himself by a pledge, he shall not break his word. He shall do according to all that proceeds out of his mouth." Originally, people viewed such oaths as completely binding on one's mortal life and soul. But as time went on, people began to make oaths in a frivolous and thoughtless way.

I have spent a great deal of time among Arabs in the Middle East, and I've heard people swear oaths for the most trivial and meaningless reasons. Once, I bargained with a tradesman for a curio worth less than two dollars. When I named the price I was willing to pay, he argued, "This is my final price. On the honor of God, I can go no lower. Already I make no profit on the sale. I swear by my God."

Now, he knew he was lying, I knew he was lying, and he knew that I knew he was lying. Eventually, he came down to a price lower than his "final price." His oath meant nothing.

Jesus taught that we should have an absolute regard for the truth. He didn't want us to put ourselves in the position of swearing to a promise that we might later be unable to keep. He didn't want us to invoke the name of God to bind our word. That's why he said in the Sermon on the Mount:

> "Again you have heard that it was said to those of old, 'You shall not swear falsely, but shall perform to the Lord what you have sworn.' But I say to you, Do not take an oath at all, either by heaven, for it is the throne of God, or by the earth, for it is his footstool, or by Jerusalem, for it is the city of the great King. And do not take an oath by your head, for you cannot make one hair white or black. Let what you say be simply 'Yes' or 'No'; anything more than this comes from evil" (Matthew 5:33-37).

Jesus always spoke the truth, but he never swore an oath. He let the facts speak for themselves. He didn't waste time trying to convince the inconvincible. He didn't plead with people to believe him. He didn't make extravagant claims. When the disciples realized that he was the Messiah who had been promised in the Old Testament, it wasn't because he told the disciples, "I am the Messiah." They realized who he was because his works spoke for him.

The opponents of Jesus accused him of many things. They said that he blasphemed when he made himself equal with God. They accused him of working miracles by demonic power. They attacked him for breaking the Sabbath when he healed on the Sabbath day. But they never attacked him for lying, because they could never catch him in a lie. Jesus told the truth…in every way…and all the time.

Speaking the Truth in Love

It's not enough to merely speak the truth. How we speak the truth matters.

Some people use "the truth" as a weapon. They can't wait to tell someone an ugly truth, because they are eager to inflict hurt or cause division. They love to give their opinions, then say, "Well, I'm just being truthful. I don't believe in beating around the bush."

Christians are not called merely to speak the truth. As the apostle Paul writes, "Rather, speaking the truth in love, we are to grow up in every way into him who is the head, into Christ" (Ephesians 4:15). There is a big difference—indeed, all the difference in the world—between merely speaking the truth and speaking the truth in love.

When we use the truth to hurt others, or to divide friend from friend, or to belittle or degrade someone, we are using the truth maliciously and sinfully. When we speak the truth in love, God's Spirit speaks through us. Sometimes the truth does hurt, and we can't avoid that. But we can make sure that our motives for speaking the truth are pure, godly, and righteous.

Someone once said to me, "The Holy Spirit is a gentleman. A gentleman never behaves rudely or unkindly." I believe that's true. God clothes his truth in kindness. When Jesus came into the world, he not only brought truth into the world, but he was "full of grace and truth" (see John 1:14). When we are called upon to speak the truth, let us always clothe the truth in love and grace.

For some leaders, lying holds no temptation. But most of us find it easy to misuse the truth, to compromise the truth, to stretch the truth, or to speak the truth with the wrong motives and without love. The leadership style of Jesus reminds us that authentic leaders must always speak the truth, always live the truth, and always handle the truth with love.

When Jesus spoke the truth, some people were attracted, but many people were repelled. Once, when he spoke the truth, the crowds deserted him (see John 6:66). He could have made himself more popular by shading the truth or stretching the truth. But Jesus *is* the truth. He could not deny the truth because he could not deny himself.

You may be struggling to live out the truth in your leadership life. Your struggle to speak the truth in love as a leader may be never-ending. The temptation to compromise the truth or compromise love may always be with you. If so, it's a battle worth fighting daily. As you battle to maintain the truth, the One who is the way, the truth, and the life is always with you, always on your side.

This leads us to our next principle:

Principle 8

Authentic leaders love the truth,
and they speak the truth in love.

9   Forgiveness

On November 14, 1940, the German Luftwaffe bombed the city of Coventry, England. Lasting almost ten hours, it was the longest air raid over Britain during World War II. When the bombing ended, residents surveyed the devastation and saw that their beautiful cathedral had been bombed to rubble.

Some of the residents refused to turn their place of worship into an excuse for revenge and bitterness. The day after the bombing, members of the congregation found two charred roof beams, fastened them together in the form of a cross, and set them up at the east end of the ruins, where the altar had been. Then they placed a sign at the foot of the cross that read, "Father Forgive."

I have a replica of that cross in my home. The original cross was later moved and now stands next to the reconstructed cathedral. I hope it will stand there as long as human civilization lasts, a reminder to the world that even in the midst of human hate and the devastation of war, we can still echo the words of Jesus, "Father, forgive them, for they know not what they do" (Luke 23:34).

The first Christians learned forgiveness from the example of Jesus himself. At the darkest moment of the Lord's life, he pleaded with the Father to forgive his executioners. Sometime later, the first Christian martyr Stephen prayed a nearly identical prayer as he was being stoned to death by his persecutors: "Lord, do not hold this sin against them" (Acts 7:60).

Authentic forgiveness not only says, "I hold nothing against you," but it also wants the guilty person to be forgiven by God as well. We sometimes find it hard to ask that and really mean it. But as Stephen demonstrated, it is possible for a Christian to have that same Christ-like, forgiving spirit, even while suffering incredible pain, hatred, and injustice.

Jesus taught us the necessity of forgiveness when he showed his disciples how to pray. Whenever we pray the Lord's Prayer, we need to be careful not to simply recite it by rote. When praying that prayer, we should always think about the words and speak them with absolute sincerity—or we should not speak them at all:

> "Our Father in heaven,
> hallowed be your name.
> Your kingdom come,
> your will be done,
>   on earth as it is in heaven.
> Give us this day our daily bread,
> and forgive us our debts,
>   as we also have forgiven our debtors.
> And lead us not into temptation,
>   but deliver us from evil."
>
>   (Matthew 6:9-13)

The message of this prayer is that we are asking God to forgive us in exactly the same way we forgive others. But do we really want God to forgive us that way? If we want God to give grace to us, shouldn't we gladly give grace to others?

How to Forgive

God, in both the Old Testament and the New Testament, commands his people to practice forgiveness. God never commands us to do anything we can't do.

I remember when I first understood the phrase "and forgive us our debts, as we also have forgiven our debtors." I had been pondering what it means to forgive other people, when suddenly it hit me: I can truly understand how to forgive others only when I myself know what it means to be forgiven.

Jesus, citing Leviticus 19:18, said, "You shall love your neighbor as yourself" (Matthew 22:39). This is a very high standard. We know what it's like to love ourselves. We take care of our own needs, feed ourselves, cleanse ourselves, take care of our appearance, provide for our comfort and pleasure, and seek the best for ourselves. Now God, in both the Old and New Testaments, tells us that we must love others with the same care and attention.

God knows we need to experience love in order to express love, so he tells us that we should love others in the same way that we love ourselves. This same principle applies to forgiveness. In order to express forgiveness to others, we need to experience forgiveness. Those who have received Jesus as Savior and Lord have truly experienced forgiveness. We know how forgiveness feels, and we are better equipped to express that forgiveness to others.

In his late-night conversation with Nicodemus the Pharisee, Jesus explained why and how God forgives us:

> "For God so loved the world, that he gave his only Son,
> that whoever believes in him should not perish but have
> eternal life. For God did not send his Son into the world
> to condemn the world, but in order that the world might
> be saved through him" (John 3:16-17).

God loves the creatures he created—the human race, you and me. He provided for our salvation through Jesus Christ. God's love is the "why" of forgiveness. His Son Jesus is the "how" of forgiveness.

The story of the woman caught in the act of adultery, which we looked at in a previous chapter, shows us God's forgiveness in action (see John 8:1-11). Jesus told her, "Neither do I condemn you; go, and from now on sin no more." In one sense, that is an uplifting story. After all, what could be more uplifting than to have all your sins forgiven?

But at the same time, the story also discourages us. Remember the Lord's instruction to this woman: "from now on sin no more." And he meant just that: *never again*. The Scriptures do not tell us the outcome of this woman's life, but I would like to believe she never committed adultery again.

But what about other sins? Did this woman go for the rest of her life without ever telling a lie? Without coveting someone else's possessions? Without behaving selfishly? Without losing her temper? I'm sure she must have sinned, even though Jesus told her not to. What then? Would Jesus have to forgive her a second time?

In 1 John 2:1, the apostle John writes, "My little children, I am writing these things to you so that you may not sin. But if anyone does sin, we have an advocate with the Father, Jesus Christ the righteous." This verse expresses God's will for his people at all times: don't sin. But if anyone does sin, there is a remedy. There is grace. There is forgiveness. It comes through Jesus the righteous, our advocate before the Father.

That is the principle of forgiveness. God opposes sin. He hates sin. He wants to root sin out of our lives. But God knows our fallen nature, and he makes a way for us to be reconciled to him when we sin.

As leaders following the leadership style of Jesus, opposing sin in our lives and the lives of those who follow us is a must. Yet we also must offer forgiveness and a pathway to mend the relationship and restore the sinner to a place of usefulness and wholeness.

Forgiving and Forgetting

To forgive is to erase a wrong.

Once, a long time ago, a man hurt me deeply by something he said. Years later someone mentioned that man's name, and I remembered that he had hurt me and that I had forgiven him. For a few seconds, I tried to recall exactly what he had said that had been so hurtful—but I couldn't.

Then the thought hit me: *I don't need to remember. I have already forgiven him!*

I silently gave thanks to God for erasing the memory of that hurt. I was grateful that I could remember nothing but the important part—the matter was resolved and forgiven.

We all suffer hurts and wounds from the actions of others. I have learned that I have truly forgiven when my pain over the wrong has begun to subside and I no longer feel an inner turmoil over the situation. When I can talk about the incident and not feel my stomach tighten or my voice become constricted, I know that forgiveness has begun healing the hurt.

I've heard people say, "I'll forgive you, but I'll never forget." I wonder what they think they are achieving by refusing to forget. Are we really practicing forgiveness if we choose never to forget? As long as we keep turning the memory over in our minds, we keep the fire of pain and bitterness burning. Choosing to forget, choosing to let go of that memory whenever it comes up, is how we put the fire out.

I once heard a woman named Eunice, a former missionary to Liberia, tell a story about forgiveness, and that story has remained with me ever since. An African man worked for her, and one day she caught him stealing clothes from her house.

"Please forgive me," he pleaded. "I did wrong, but I promise I will never do it again."

She forgave the man and allowed him to continue working for her. Less than a month passed before she caught him stealing again.

"Look at what you've done," she said. "You've stolen from me again!"

"What kind of Christian are you?" the man replied.

Eunice was dumbfounded. "What do you mean?"

"If you truly forgave me, then you do not remember that I stole from you before. And if you do not remember, then it never happened."

The man's logic was self-serving, to say the least. He was presuming on Eunice's forgiveness to rationalize his sin. Nevertheless, there is a certain element of validity in what he says. When we forgive someone, we should seek to forget. Obviously, forgiveness does not afflict us with amnesia. To some degree, we can't help remembering hurts that we have recently experienced.

But we can, with God's help, make an effort to forgive and forget. Whenever we remember a hurt, we have a choice to make: Will I dwell on that hurt, turn it over in my mind, and reexperience the bitterness of it again and again—or will I set it aside, mentally change the subject, and ask God for the grace to let go of that memory?

A Mark of Leadership

At the height of the American Civil War, President Abraham Lincoln spoke at an official White House reception. In his remarks, he said that the southerners of the Confederacy should be thought of as erring human beings, not as enemies to be exterminated. An elderly Yankee woman with a fiery temper rebuked President Lincoln for speaking kindly about his enemies. "You ought to be thinking of how to destroy them," she said.

"Why, madam," President Lincoln replied, "do I not destroy my enemies when I make them my friends?"[1]

Effective leaders are forgiving leaders. We cannot work with people by holding grudges against them. Here are three suggestions for ways to build a more Christlike and forgiving spirit into your leadership style:

1. Self-Examination

Sometimes it is helpful to ask ourselves why we are holding a grudge and refusing to forgive and forget. A friend once said to me, "You are the only person who can truly hurt your feelings. Other people can touch a tender part of your life that you have not yet surrendered to Jesus Christ, but you make the choice whether to hold on to that hurt or let it go."

Other people sometimes say or do things that trigger a childhood sense of inferiority or insecurity or a fear of not measuring up to expectations. People often don't mean to hurt us. They accidentally set off an emotional landmine inside us. These experiences show us that we need to do some emotional housekeeping, asking God to heal those areas of hurt.

Instead of being bitter and angry toward those who have stepped on our emotional toes, let's forgive and ask God to shine a healing light on those dark corners of our souls. Let's allow God to transform those wounds into insight and understanding so that we can free ourselves from the pain of the past.

2. Prayer

Pray especially for your enemies. Write down the names of people you struggle to forgive. Lift them up to God every day. Don't pray, "God please convict this person and bring him to his senses." Instead, pray, "Father, help me to understand this person. Help me to love and forgive this person, and to truly want the best for him. Give me a heart full of Christlike love and compassion for him." It's hard to be bitter toward someone you're praying for.

3. Effort and Expectation

Healing doesn't just happen. We have to work at it and expect it to happen. We have to approach the hurts in our lives with an open attitude that says, "God, use my wounds for your glory. Use my hurts to make me a better servant. Use the mistreatment I suffer to enable me to understand others and empathize with their hurts. Father, I know you are going to heal me and help me to forgive. Thank you for what you are doing in my life."

If we actively work toward reconciliation, forgiveness, and healing, and if we expect God to answer that prayer, it will happen. God will bring healing to our deepest hurts.

Edith Cavell was a British nurse who helped establish a nursing school in Brussels, Belgium, in 1907. When World War I broke out in 1914, Germany marched into Belgium and occupied the country. The hospital and nursing school where Edith served became a Red Cross hospital in a war zone. In the course of the war, wounded British and French soldiers—prisoners of the German army—would be brought to the Red Cross hospital for treatment. Wounded German soldiers were also treated there, and Edith gave equally compassionate care and treatment to soldiers from both sides.

But Edith Cavell was a patriot, and she worked with the Belgian resistance to help British and French soldiers escape to the Netherlands, a neutral country. She also facilitated the escape of many Belgian men of military age, who would otherwise have been forced to serve as soldiers in the German army.

A French soldier who was treated at the hospital later turned out to be collaborating with the Germans. He betrayed Edith Cavell, and the Germans arrested her in August 1915. After a trial lasting only two days, she was convicted of treason (even though she was a foreign national), and sentenced to die before a firing squad on the morning of October 12.

The night before her execution, an Anglican chaplain, the Reverend Stirling Gahan, visited Edith Cavell at the prison and gave her Holy Communion. He later reported that her last words were, "Patriotism is not enough. I must have no hatred or bitterness toward anyone."[2]

Those are not just the words of a Red Cross nurse. Those are the forgiving words of an authentic leader who lived and died by the leadership style of Jesus. This brings us to our next leadership principle:

Principle 9

Authentic leaders forgive
because they have been forgiven.

Part 3

The
Temptations
of Leadership

10   Power

Jesus did everything wrong, according to the leadership wisdom of this world.

There are essentially two classic leadership models today, and the leadership style of Jesus is unquestionably the minority view. The more commonly accepted leadership model is descended from the writings of Italian politician and humanist philosopher Niccolò Machiavelli (1469–1527). In his book *The Prince*, he advocated a style of leadership rooted solely in the pursuit of power.

Machiavelli taught that leaders must be ruthless in the pursuit of power, that they should maintain an outwardly moral reputation but be willing to act immorally to maintain power. Machiavelli is credited with originating the saying, "the ends justify the means"—the notion that even immoral actions are justified if they produce a desirable outcome. According to Machiavelli, if a leader must use brutal force, deception, coercion, or the elimination of rivals in order to acquire and maintain power, then he should not hesitate to do so.

Machiavelli's *The Prince* has had a widespread influence through the centuries. Leaders who have read and adopted the leadership style of Machiavelli include England's ruthless chief minister Thomas Cromwell, who served the equally ruthless King Henry VIII (who ultimately turned on Cromwell and executed him); Spain's Charles V, a greedy and ruthless monarch who launched many wars and opposed the Protestant Reformation; Catherine de Médicis, who instigated the St. Bartholomew's Day massacre against French Protestants; the Scottish atheist philosopher David Hume; and Soviet leader Joseph Stalin, who killed millions of his own people in forced labor camps and deliberately engineered famines. (Stalin read *The Prince* many times, underlining and scribbling notes in the margins.)

To this day, a scheming leader who will do anything for the sake of power is described as "Machiavellian." Niccolò Machiavelli advocated a leadership style based on amorality, deception, power, ego, and personal advantage. By contrast, Jesus of Nazareth taught and modeled a leadership style based on morality, truthfulness, servanthood, humility, and meeting the needs of others.

Jesus started with a motley group of twelve followers. None were well-educated. Some were undoubtedly illiterate. One was a traitor. Yet with that small group, Jesus changed history and impacted the entire world. We date our calendars by his life. So I ask you, would you rather follow the leadership model of Machiavelli or the leadership style of Jesus?

Two Kinds of Power

When people think of leadership, they usually think of power. The issue of power applies to leadership in every arena of human endeavor: business, education, church, and home. Anywhere two or more people gather together to achieve a goal or purpose, power comes into play.

While Jesus did not pursue power at any cost in the way that Machiavelli advocates, he did not condemn the use of power per se. But Jesus differed from the standard secular model of leadership in the way he viewed power.

First, let's define what we mean by *power*. In a leadership context, I define power as "the ability to influence, inspire, or induce behavior in others." In leadership, there are two kinds of power: *position power* and *personal power*.

Position power refers to the influence leaders have because of the position they hold in the organization. An employee might not volunteer for a certain task if a coworker asked him to do it. But if his superior—a person with the power of position in the organization—asks him to do it, that employee will probably volunteer in a heartbeat. A powerful position gives one clout to command, motivate, and even intimidate others in the organization.

One of the leadership challenges Jesus faced as he taught and mentored the disciples was teaching them a completely new kind of leadership, a new kind of power. They thought his kingdom would be a worldly kingdom, and his power would be worldly political power.

In Matthew 20, James and John, along with their mother, take Jesus aside to ask for a favor. Their mother does the talking, asking Jesus to promise he'll give her boys positions on his right and left hand. In other words, she wanted King Jesus to make her sons the chancellor and prime minister of the kingdom. James, John, and their mother were thinking about position power. They wanted Jesus to give them the positions so they would have the power.

But as Jesus would later tell Pontius Pilate, his kingdom was not of this world. His power was not worldly power, the power of position. So Jesus told this mother and her sons, "You do not know what you are asking. Are you able to drink the cup that I am to drink?"

"We are able," they replied.

"You will drink my cup," Jesus said somberly, knowing that James and John would become martyrs for the Christian faith, "but to sit at my right hand and at my left is not mine to grant, but it is for those for whom it has been prepared by my Father."

The other ten disciples heard about what James and John and their mother had done, trying to jump to the head of the line for high positions in the coming kingdom. They too were thinking of the kingdom of Jesus as a worldly kingdom based on worldly position power.

But Jesus rebuked them all, saying, "You know that the rulers of the Gentiles lord it over them, and their great ones exercise authority over them. It shall not be so among you. But whoever would be great among you must be your servant, and whoever would be first among you must be your slave, even as the Son of Man came not to be served but to serve, and to give his life as a ransom for many" (see Matthew 20:20-28).

This was one of several instances where Jesus had to rebuke the disciples for their worldly, even Machiavellian view of leadership and power. On several occasions, he had to teach them that his leadership style is based instead on servanthood.

On another occasion, Jesus and the disciples were walking to Capernaum. The Twelve, thinking Jesus couldn't hear them, argued among themselves. But when they reached their destination, Jesus asked, "What were you discussing on the way?"

The shame-faced disciples couldn't answer, because they had argued about which among them was the greatest. So Jesus told them once again that his style of leadership was not about who was the greatest or who had the top position. "If anyone would be first," Jesus said, "he must be last of all and servant of all" (see Mark 9:33-35).

Over and over, Jesus taught his disciples this new and paradoxical form of leadership: In the kingdom of Jesus, the leader is the one who serves, and the servant is the one who leads. Jesus came to stand position power on its head.

Personal power comes from one's charisma and personality. A leader who projects confidence, strength, hope, optimism, and sincerity can always inspire people through personal power, even in seemingly hopeless situations.

In May 1940, during the darkest days of World War II, British Prime Minister Winston Churchill stood before the House of Commons and delivered a speech that was broadcast by radio to the entire nation. In the course of that speech, he said these words:

"I have nothing to offer but blood, toil, tears, and sweat. We have before us an ordeal of the most grievous kind. We have before us many, many long months of struggle and of suffering."

Those are dark and depressing words, and Churchill was giving the British people a realistic assessment of the crisis they faced. As ink on paper, those words cause the soul to sink into despair. Yet, when spoken by Churchill, those words actually had the effect of lifting the morale and igniting the fighting spirit of the British people.

With his bulldog swagger, Churchill went on to say, "You ask, what is our aim? I can answer in one word: Victory. Victory at all costs, victory in spite of all terror, victory, however long and hard the road may be, for without victory there is no survival."

Winston Churchill did not sugarcoat the problems they faced. He communicated the enormity of the crisis in no uncertain terms—but he focused on the task ahead through the lens of his personal power, his infectious confidence, his defiant courage. And the result was that a seemingly defeated nation experienced a resurgent morale. The people of Great Britain rallied behind him, battled bravely, and fulfilled his promise of victory.

Of course, there is always a danger in personal power. In our media age, there is the increasing possibility that we will give power and influence to demagogues—to skilled manipulators with superficial charm but without the experience, ability, values, and character that make an authentic leader. There are already many superficially charming people who are distorting popular opinion on our TV screens, producing distorted policy and legislation in Washington, DC, and even distorting God's truth in pulpits across the country.

Charming, manipulative leaders can acquire tyrannical powers. It happened in Germany in the 1930s, when a man with a gift of persuasive oratory led Nazi Germany—and the entire world—into global war. It happened in a different way in 1978 when a charming and manipulative preacher named Jim Jones led nearly a thousand followers, including two hundred children, to death by mass murder-suicide in Jonestown, Guyana.

Personal power can be a great force for good when wielded by a great leader like Winston Churchill. But personal power cannot be trusted. Those who charm us with their personal magnetism, those who sway us with their persuasive words, may be very effective leaders, but where are they leading us? Personal power sometimes leads to destruction.

The Five Power Plays

Worldly leaders employ a number of techniques to maintain their power. They will use position power, personal power, or a combination of both in order to manipulate people and achieve their ends. They generally maintain power through what I call "The Five Power Plays." Let's examine these Power Plays one by one.

Power Play 1: Manipulation

The infamous Jim Jones of Jonestown stands out as an example of manipulation because he led so many people to a bizarre and sensational death by mass suicide. People look at that awful event in 1978 and say, "I don't know how Jim Jones was able to manipulate so many people. He could never brainwash *me* into accepting such a fate!"

But is anyone truly immune to the power of manipulation of a charismatic personality? Jim Jones was, after all, a preacher and the founder of a large religious movement, the People's Temple. He adopted children, preached a social gospel of racial tolerance, and set up outreach programs for the poor. He gained credibility by associating with prominent politicians such as San Francisco Mayor George Moscone (who appointed him chairman of the Housing Authority Commission), First Lady Rosalynn Carter, and Vice President Walter Mondale. Outwardly, Jim Jones had an aura of respectability on a national stage and was considered a pillar of the community.

Jones attracted crowds of followers to his People's Temple—and he used methods of manipulation to keep them there. He played on people's fears, warning against a coming nuclear apocalypse. Authentic leaders motivate and inspire their followers with truth, logic, facts, and reason, while manipulators like Jim Jones use fear and irrational emotion to keep people in line. Manipulators are psychological bullies who intimidate insecure people with lines like, "You don't want people to think you are uncooperative and not giving your best to God, do you?" Or "People tell me that you're a troublemaker, and I want you to prove them wrong." Jim Jones always knew the right words to say to silence objections and keep people under his thumb.

It's instructive to note that Jim Jones used the same manipulative tactics that the leaders of the Pharisee cult used in Jesus's day. In John 7, the Pharisees, the bitter enemies of Jesus, wanted to arrest Jesus and do away with him without trial. Nicodemus, the Pharisee who had earlier visited Jesus by night, protested, "Does our law judge a man without first giving him a hearing and learning what he does?"

Enraged, the other Pharisees ganged up on him and replied, "Are you from Galilee too?" The Judean Jews looked down on the Galileans, and the not-too-subtle implication of that question was that if Nicodemus defended Jesus the Galilean, they might treat Nicodemus as a Galilean as well. They didn't have to use an open threat—a single question was sufficiently intimidating. Nicodemus said no more in defense of Jesus.

That is how manipulators get their way and maintain their power.

Power Play 2: Guilt or Shame

Leaders, by virtue of their powerful positions, have the ability to induce feelings of guilt and shame in their subordinates and followers. Abusive leaders often manipulate people with guilt feelings in order to maintain control over them.

Take, for example, this story from a woman named Jessie who worked in an office in New York City:

> I always feel stupid in front of my boss. The other day, when I walked into the office in my running shoes, he asked me why I was wearing them. I told him I had power-walked to work. He said, "Do people still power-walk in New York City?" I laughed at his comment but couldn't believe I said something so stupid. I wanted to crawl in a hole. I can never say anything smart in front of the boss. I feel like he thinks I'm just some stupid girl in the office. [1]

Do you see what happened here? Jessie's boss asked her a seemingly innocent question—yet that one question filled Jessie with self-doubt, shame, and feelings of inferiority. There's nothing stupid about power-walking. It's a perfectly legitimate form of exercise that is still practiced in New York City and all across the country. But this boss knew exactly how to twist the verbal knife and make Jessie doubt herself and feel insecure. Maybe this boss didn't know the effect his words had on Jessie, yet from her words it is clear that this was not the first conversation in which he had made her feel shame. I think it's safe to conclude that this was a manipulative power play this boss regularly used to keep an employee off balance and under his control.

Power Play 3: Intimidation

In his book *Toxic Emotions at Work*, Peter Frost relates the story of a corporate CEO who ruled by fear and intimidation. At meetings with his senior managers, he would invariably select one person as his victim, and he would verbally attack that person for several minutes. "The CEO seemed to be intentionally setting a tone,"

Frost wrote, "creating a level of fear and intimidation in the group that carried over into the agenda discussions."

On another occasion, that same CEO conducted the firing of one of his senior managers as a symbolic public hanging. First, he tipped off the rest of the staff that the firing would take place. Then he went into the manager's glass-walled office so that all the staff would be able to watch the drama from their own desks in the open office. When the abusive CEO began his rant, the manager asked that they go to a private office and conduct the rest of the discussion in a confidential setting. The CEO refused and continued haranguing and humiliating the man in front of his friends and peers. Then he punctuated the discussion by telling the man he was fired.

Clearly, the CEO's goal was to instill fear throughout his organization as a means of demonstrating his power and control. Peter Frost concludes that the CEO's plan backfired because "many of the staff members were angered and demoralized by the spectacle." The result of that fear-inducing symbolic public hanging was a "chain reaction of poorer performance and general discontent"—the exact opposite of the effect the CEO was trying to achieve. [2]

Richard D. Parsons, former CEO of Time Warner, recalled one boss he had early in his career—a boss who intimidated others with his explosive temper. On one occasion, the volatile boss blew up during a meeting, yelled at one employee and even threw things at the unfortunate man. The worst moment came when the victim— a grown man—broke down and cried in front of everyone in the room.

For Parsons, it was a powerful lesson that intimidation undermines the entire organization. The fear factor, Parsons concluded, "tended to stifle, muffle, and impede effective communications, particularly bad news...No one wanted to set off this manager, so they didn't tell him things they thought he wouldn't be happy hearing." [3]

By contrast, the most successful companies are often led by the kindest and most caring of CEOs. One example is the Atlanta-based

Chick-fil-A restaurant chain, founded in 1946 by Christian busi-nessman S. Truett Cathy, who built his reputation on the leadership style of Jesus. He has always put faith, integrity, and people ahead of profits (for example, his restaurants are always closed on Sundays, giving his employees a biblical day of rest).

In an interview on Fox News Channel, host Neil Cavuto said, "Mr. Cathy, they say you can't be a nice guy in this business. It's a rough world, you have to be tough. What do you say?"

"Well," Cathy replied, "I think the opposite. I think the kinder you are to your people, the more productive they will be and the more customers you will be able to attract. I think I kind of look upon being in the restaurant business as a divine calling."[4]

Power Play 4: Ridicule

I define ridicule as using humor as a weapon to hurt people. A sense of humor is a powerful and positive tool in the hands of an authentic, Christlike leader. But in the hands of an abusive, control-ling boss or tyrant, humor becomes a weapon of control, usually in the form of mockery and ridicule.

Historian J. Michael Waller of the Institute of World Politics tells us that ridicule was a favorite technique of Adolf Hitler for main-taining control of his underlings—though the Führer himself could not take a joke. "Hitler's sense of humor knew no self-deprecation," Waller writes. "His was what the Germans call *schadenfreude*…tak-ing malicious pleasure at others' misfortune. Hitler loved cruel jokes on his own ministers, especially on Foreign Minister Ribbentrop… He could never laugh at himself."[5]

Professor Bennett Tepper of Georgia State University conducted research on employees who worked for abusive bosses. His study involved more than seven hundred adults who worked at private, public, and nonprofit workplaces. His findings, as reported by researcher Robert I. Sutton at the University of California at Berke-ley, revealed many of these people "had bosses who used ridicule, put-downs, the silent treatment, and insults…These demeaning acts drove people to quit their jobs at higher rates and sapped the effectiveness of those who remained." Employees who stayed on the job felt "reduced commitment to employers, and heightened depression, anxiety, and burnout."[6]

Sometimes, leaders can fall into the trap of using the power play of ridicule without even realizing it. A friend told me about a lesson he learned while working one Christmas season at a hostel for international students. A jolly and good-natured fellow, my friend seemed to work well with students from other cultures.

But one day two Middle Eastern young men said to him, "You smile a lot, and that means you are happy and cooperative, does it not? And you say we do not have to go on some of the trips you have arranged. And you say it with a smile. But if we do not go, you also say words that make us know we have displeased and disappointed you. All the while, you continue smiling, even when you say things like, 'You're not too tired to go.' Please forgive us, but we don't understand."

My friend instantly realized his error—and regretted it. On one level, he wanted everyone to attend every function, even though he told the students they didn't have to. In an attempt to manipulate them into going, he would use a humorous jab, delivered with a smile, which he thought would soften the jab. Instead, the conflicting mixture of verbal and nonverbal messages he sent was confusing to the students.

"I learned a valuable lesson," he told me. "I never realized before how I used a smile and belittling humor to get my way with people."

A good sense of humor is an important leadership trait. If you read the gospels objectively, you find that Jesus had a finely tuned Middle Eastern sense of humor. He loved hyperbole, creating ridiculous word pictures to make a point while making his listeners laugh. The image of someone obsessing over a speck in his neighbor's eye while ignoring a huge plank in his own eye is as funny as it is instructive. He also used word pictures of a camel trying to squeeze through the eye of a needle, and compared the absurd legalism of the Pharisees to straining a gnat out of one's drink, then swallowing a camel. In arguments, he used devastating logic and wit to expose the irrationality of his opponents' accusations.

But Jesus never used humor to belittle, shame, ridicule, or mock his followers. He always used humor to instruct and to build relationships. That's the leadership style of Jesus, and it's the model we should follow in our own leadership lives.

Power Play 5: Emotional Appeals

There's nothing wrong with involving the emotions of your audience as long as your message is honest and supported by facts and reason. But all too often, when a leader doesn't have truth and logic on his side, he resorts to tricking his audience with emotional appeals. This is a ruthless power play that is unworthy of the leadership style of Jesus, whose message was always rooted in truth.

A prime example of a manipulative emotional appeal is the phrase "for the children." This phrase is known as a "thought-terminating cliché" because it can be invoked to shut down a rational debate. We are all "for the children," and we all want the best for all children, especially our own. Jesus himself was a caring advocate for children (see Matthew 18:3; 19:13-14; Mark 10:13-14; Luke 18:15-16). So there is nothing wrong with a leader expressing honest caring and concern for children.

What is manipulative and dishonest is when our so-called leaders prey on our love for children and manipulate us with emotional appeals. When politicians want to expand their power by raising our taxes, they tell us that budget cuts would cause schools to decline, and kids would no longer have textbooks, pencils, and school lunches for their hungry bellies—as if there were not a dime of fat to be trimmed in the rest of the budget.

Meanwhile, the taxes we already pay are being raided by these very same politicians through fraud, graft, payoffs, and cronyism. After the people vote themselves higher taxes, supposedly "for the children," the children will be no better off than they were before—but the politicians and the special interests will be richer than ever.

The "for the children" appeal is often used to change the subject when a leader gets in trouble. A few years ago a presidential candidate got into trouble because of some unsavory associations in his past. So his wife went on NBC's *Today* show to make an emotional appeal that we all stop talking about her husband's unwholesome connections and focus instead on the needs of "the children." She told the interviewer, "We've got to move forward. You know, this conversation doesn't help my kids. It doesn't help kids out there who are looking for us to make decisions and choices about how we're going to better fund education."

It was a classic thought-terminating cliché, a case of misdirection, as when a magician gestures with his right hand so you don't notice the card up his left sleeve. "Stop talking about scandal and talk about educating kids instead. Do it for the children." Her emotional appeal, while effective, actually turns logic on its head. If we really care about children, we should be *very* concerned about the character and associations of the person who is going to lead our nation and ultimately influence our kids' education. Manipulative emotional appeals have a tendency to lead people to mistaken conclusions.

Manipulators and con men tug at our heartstrings to control us and gain power over us. But Jesus, the quintessential leader, always told the truth and appealed to the intellect and the will. He told his followers, "If you abide in my word, you are truly my disciples, and you will know the truth, and the truth will set you free" (John 8:31b-32).

How Jesus Answered Power

In John 13, we see Jesus, hours before the crucifixion, wrapping a towel around his waist, filling a basin with water, and washing the feet of the disciples. Washing feet was a job for the lowest servant in the household. Jesus taught by his words and his example that those who would lead must be servants to their followers.

Jesus showed us that the way up is down, the master is the servant, the greatest is the least, and the way to exaltation is to take up one's cross daily and follow Jesus (see Luke 9:23). Whereas Niccolò Machiavelli taught that leadership is a ruthless and relentless quest for power, Jesus taught that leadership is servanthood. The leadership model of this world is based on control, manipulation, and fear. The leadership model of Jesus is based on a love that casts out fear (see 1 John 4:18).

After washing the feet of his disciples, Jesus said to them, "A new commandment I give to you, that you love one another: just as I have loved you, you also are to love one another. By this all people will know that you are my disciples, if you have love for one another" (John 13:34-35).

Jesus rejected the world's definition of power. He did not seek power by manipulating and controlling people. He derived his power from God. He exercised that power through love. He extended his power to his followers and safeguarded that power against abuse by commanding his followers to love one another. A leader who loves his people will never manipulate or exploit them. He will seek only what is best for them.

The most widely recognized symbol of Christianity is the cross. It's a wonderful symbol because it speaks of obedience and love—the obedience of Jesus to God the Father and the love of Jesus for lost humanity.

But there is another symbol of Christianity that we rarely see: the symbol of the basin and towel. This is the symbol of humble Christian service. The basin and towel are the tools of the Servant-Leader who washed his followers' feet. All of these symbols are marks of Christian leadership because they stand for the leadership style of

Jesus—his humility, his servanthood, his obedience, and his love. These symbols suggest to us our next leadership principle:

Principle 10

Authentic leaders derive their greatest power
from obeying God and serving others.

11   Ego

A well-known speaker agreed to speak at an annual gathering of a major organization. The day of the event, he arrived and registered like any other attendee, received a name tag, and then proceeded to wander around the hall. No one recognized him. No one paid any attention to him.

When he got up to speak, he began with some caustic remarks expressing his disappointment that no one had welcomed him on his arrival. I spoke to him after the event, and he told me his feelings were hurt because he had gone unrecognized.

"I wanted to walk out of the place," he said. "The event organizers had told me over the phone how eager they were to have me come and speak, but when I arrived, I felt totally let down."

The human ego is fragile and easily offended. Our egos often get in the way of effective, Christlike leadership.

Jesus was never upset when people failed to recognize him. In fact, he usually avoided publicity and recognition.

On one occasion, the disciple Philip urged his friend Nathanael to come and meet Jesus. When Nathanael learned where Jesus came from, he replied, "Can anything good come out of Nazareth?"

It was an insult—yet Jesus never rebuked Nathanael for that slur. Even though the fame of Jesus had spread far and wide, he showed no sign of being offended that he was not recognized or respected. He talked to Nathanael, and at the end of their conversation,

Nathanael exclaimed, "Rabbi, you are the Son of God! You are the King of Israel!" (see John 1:46-51).

Read through the gospels and you'll see that Jesus never blurted, "I am the Messiah!" In fact, you don't find him even hinting at who he was. He concentrated on teaching, preaching, and demonstrating his purpose for coming, and then he allowed people to draw their own conclusions.

When Jesus traveled from village to village, he did not expect to be greeted by banners, reception committees, or honors. His ego did not seek the fulfillment that comes from the applause of the crowds. He specifically said, "I do not receive glory from people" (John 5:41).

When the disciples offered him food as he sat beside a well in Samaria, Jesus said, "My food is to do the will of him who sent me and to accomplish his work" (John 4:34). Jesus was not saying that he never became physically hungry. Rather, he was saying that he subordinated his physical needs to the all-important mission his Father had given him. By this leadership example, he taught his disciples that their mission in life was also to do the will of God the Father, not feed their own egos.

Jesus came as a servant, not a celebrity. Leadership requires us to recognize what we have to do, then roll up our sleeves and do it. We don't need to be applauded, recognized, or celebrated for it. As servants, we simply need to get our work done. If we expect recognition and praise for doing the Father's will, we have ceased to think of ourselves as servants. We have ceased to follow the leadership style of Jesus.

Who Gets the Credit?

A Christian woman worked in a secular publishing house. She held the title of editorial assistant, and she would read manuscripts after her editor had finished with them, checking for grammatical and punctuation errors.

The editor, her immediate superior, was incompetent at her job, but she maintained a false image of competence by relying on the assistant to clean up her mistakes. She knew the assistant was more skilled than she was, so she gave the assistant more and more of the actual work while taking the credit for herself.

One day, the editor got into an argument with her boss, the publisher. "If you don't meet my demands," the editor said, "I'll resign."

"Then I'll accept your resignation," the publisher said. "I happen to know that your assistant is doing most of your job anyway."

The editor was furious. "Did she tell you that?"

"She didn't have to. I've been aware of this situation for months, and I was wondering if you were ever going to give her the credit she deserves."

The editor left the company, and the assistant was promoted to editor. She did her work well, expecting no acknowledgment.

The publisher, who was not a Christian, took the newly promoted editor aside one day and said, "You always work so hard, yet you never demand to be recognized. Why is that?"

"Well, I suppose it's because I'm living to be obedient to the Lord. The Bible says that I'm to work heartily, as for the Lord and not for men, and that he's the one who will reward me. I knew what my old boss was doing, but I made a decision before God that I would do my best work and let God take care of who gets the credit."

The amazed publisher said, "I don't know much about religion, but I do know this: if anyone in this world is a Christian, you are."

That is leading by the leadership style of Jesus. It is a leadership model that is focused on serving God, not serving one's own ego.

Recognition Is a Two-Way Street

Authentic leaders are eager to give recognition where recognition is due. They don't want to steal credit from those who have truly earned it. They want to share credit and encourage others. They understand that all leadership accomplishments are team accomplishments, because leaders are people who achieve goals through people.

Games are won by teams not coaches. Profits are earned by companies not CEOs. Battles are won by armies not generals. Ministry is done by churches not pastors. A leader who takes sole credit for the accomplishments of a team or organization is a leader with an ego problem.

I'm not advocating false humility. If a leader earns a few moments in the limelight, that's OK. There is nothing wrong with an appropriate amount of recognition, and leaders should not feign humility for the sake of appearing humble. That's just a different kind of pride—the kind of pride that says, "Look how humble I am!"

No matter what our leadership arena may be—whether we lead a business, a platoon, a team, a church, a law firm, or a household—we are serving Jesus Christ. If we seek glory and applause from other people, we will not receive glory and approval from God. Performing to win praise from others is performing for the wrong motives.

Does it bother you when your work is not recognized? Does it annoy you when others get the credit for what you do? Does a lack of recognition and credit make you want to leave your job? Jesus led without any expectation of recognition. If you truly wish to lead by the leadership style of Jesus, then you must check your ego at the door.

The Secure Leader

Whenever someone assumes a leadership role, that person agrees, either verbally or tacitly, to expend his best efforts for the organization. As the apostle Paul put it, "Moreover, it is required of stewards that they be found faithful" (1 Corinthians 4:2).

An authentic leader cannot be insecure. He or she cannot be continually fearful of losing the leadership position. Leaders must be confident of God's leading in their lives and confident in the gifts and abilities God has given them. Insecure leaders tend to fear making decisions and frequently second-guess the few decisions they do make.

Confident leaders are decisive without being arrogant and secure without being smug. They act decisively and don't obsess over decisions once they're made. If it turns out that they made the wrong decision, then they correct the old decision with a new one and keep moving forward. That's how secure, confident leaders lead. They have learned to follow the counsel of the apostle Paul:

> Do not be anxious about anything, but in everything
> by prayer and supplication with thanksgiving let your
> requests be made known to God. And the peace of God,
> which surpasses all understanding, will guard your hearts
> and your minds in Christ Jesus (Philippians 4:6-7).

That kind of peace, confidence, and security comes from knowing who we truly serve, Jesus the Master. Leaders who live to please Jesus instead of pleasing other people have far less stress and anxiety to deal with. When we adopt the leadership style of Jesus, we feel secure knowing that we are servants of a Master who is gracious, forgiving, and accepting, a Master who understands us better than we understand ourselves.

Because we are secure in our standing before Jesus, we don't feel threatened by competition. We don't feel we have a position to protect or a reputation to defend. Jesus is our protector and our defender. We can leave everything in his hands and feel completely secure.

Phil and Steve Mahre are twin brothers and retired alpine ski racers who competed in the 1984 Winter Olympics in Sarajevo. Phil is the older of the two by four minutes. The Mahre brothers are regarded as two of the greatest American skiers of all time. During the late seventies and early eighties, they frequently competed against each other on the World Cup circuit, yet neither felt threatened by the other. They believed that competing against each other made them both better skiers.

In the 1984 Olympic finals, Phil skied before his brother and was holding first place. When Steve's turn came, Phil got on the walkie-talkie and told his brother what to expect on the way down, including a treacherously slick patch near the bottom. Why would Phil help his brother—who was, after all, a competitor—and jeopardize his own gold medal? Because Phil felt secure. His ego was strong enough that he could compete against Steve while also being a friend and supporter to his brother. He genuinely wanted his brother to turn in his best possible performance, even if it meant that Phil would take home the silver rather than the gold.

When Steve skied, he finished just 0.21 seconds behind his brother. At the awards ceremony, they stood side by side, Phil wearing the gold medal around his neck and Steve wearing the silver. Phil later recalled, "After I received the gold medal, my dad congratulated me, then he said, 'Half of that medal is your brother's.' And he was right."

Spoken like a true leader. Authentic leaders do not have fragile egos. They are secure and confident, and they do not fear competition. This brings us to our next leadership principle:

Principle 11

Genuine leaders are secure in Jesus Christ
and have no need to protect or defend their egos.

12   Anger

Over a period of weeks, a group of Christians had been witnessing to a Muslim acquaintance. The Christians and the Muslim questioned each other, listened to each other, and exchanged views and beliefs. One day, the Muslim asked the Christians a challenging question.

"Why is it," he said, "when I yell at my children, you criticize me for being angry? But when you Christians yell, you call it 'righteous indignation.' Why is my anger sin and your anger righteous?"

The Christians had no answer.

I've heard this same question raised concerning the actions of the Lord Jesus when he cleared the temple and chased out the money changers. We don't criticize Jesus for being angry; instead, we say that he was filled with righteous indignation.

What's the difference between sinful anger and righteous indignation? And what role should anger have in a leader's life? Is anger a legitimate part of the leadership style of Jesus? And should we emulate his anger?

To answer these questions, we need to examine the incident of the clearing of the temple, as recorded in John 2. Even though John does not put a label on the emotions of Jesus in that incident, there's no mistaking his feelings: The Lord was angry, and he showed it.

Jesus undertook four specific actions in the temple that day. First, he made a whip. Second, he drove out the animals. Third, he spilled the coins of the money changers on the ground. Fourth, he overturned their tables. Nowhere else in the ministry of Jesus do we find him displaying such visible anger and expressing it in such a forceful, physical way.

Outrage in the Temple

To understand why Jesus took the action he did, we must look at the background of the practice of money changing in the temple. It begins with the Jewish tradition of Passover, the greatest of all Jewish feasts. The Law stated that every Jewish male who lived within twenty miles of Jerusalem had to attend this observance. By the first century, Jews who had been scattered all over the world came back to their ancestral land for Passover.

Josephus, in *War of the Jews*, estimates that as many as 2,700,000 people filled the city of Jerusalem during the Passover festival. Modern historians, such as E.P. Sanders, are skeptical of that claim and suggest that the number was closer to half a million. In any case, we know that the city was filled to capacity with people who had gathered to celebrate the Passover, some having traveled a great distance to be there.

The Law required every male aged nineteen and older to pay a tax so that the priests could continue making temple sacrifices. They paid the tax in either Galilean shekels or "the shekels of the sanctuary," because all other coins were considered ceremonially unclean. Currency from other nations, though accepted for trade throughout Jerusalem, could not be used in worship to God. Since pilgrims came from all over the world with their own currency, money changers sat in the temple courts making the exchange for them.

Had the rate of exchange been fair, the money changers would have provided an honorable and useful service. Instead, they charged an exorbitant premium for exchanging the money, and a portion of their profits went to paying lavish bribes to the high priests of the temple. Corruption was rampant, and the religious leaders used the authority of God to intimidate the people and extort money from them.

Sellers of sacrificial animals also set up shop in the temple court, and they too paid bribes to the religious officials. The Law allowed only perfect birds and animals to be sacrificed. When the inspectors examined the animals the worshipers brought, they almost always found some sort of blemish or flaw (because the inspectors also received a share of the bribes). So the people were forced to buy animals from the sellers and the temple court at vastly inflated prices.

These injustices were perpetrated in the name of God, and that's why Jesus was angry when he came to the temple. These thieves and oppressors had desecrated God's house. The money changers, animal sellers, and high priests were all getting rich by cheating the poor and the faithful. The situation Jesus found at the temple was exactly what the prophet Micah described:

> Hear this, you heads of the house of Jacob
>   and rulers of the house of Israel,
> who detest justice
>   and make crooked all that is straight,
> who build Zion with blood
>   and Jerusalem with iniquity.
> Its heads give judgment for a bribe;
>   its priests teach for a price;
>   its prophets practice divination for money;
> yet they lean on the LORD and say,
>   "Is not the LORD in the midst of us?
>   No disaster shall come upon us."
>   (Micah 3:9-11)

Jesus chased the merchants out of the temple court to show them that God's house was to be a house of prayer. As Jesus said in Mark 11:17, "Is it not written, 'My house shall be called a house of prayer for all the nations'? But you have made it a den of robbers."

Here Jesus makes an important point. When the temple was built, it was not constructed with a place where money changing and animal vending could be conducted. The buying and selling was apparently conducted in the Court of the Gentiles, the only area of the temple where non-Jews could enter. The Court of the Gentiles was intended to be the place where Gentiles could come to pray and meditate.

But the corrupt priests had turned the Court of the Gentiles into a den of thieves. Now the Gentiles had no place of prayer in the temple. Instead, the place that had originally been set aside for the Gentiles was filled with the constant uproar of oxen, sheep, doves, and babbling merchants hawking their wares. As Jesus said, God's house had ceased to be a house of prayer for all nations.

Jesus may have also had another reason in mind for cleansing the temple. It may have been a symbolic announcement that animal sacrifices were no longer pleasing to God. The prophet Isaiah tells us how God viewed animal sacrifices:

> "What to me is the multitude of your sacrifices?
>   says the LORD;
> "I have had enough of burnt offerings of rams
>   and the fat of well-fed beasts;
> I do not delight in the blood of bulls,
>   or of lambs, or of goats.
> When you come to appear before me,
>   who has required of you
>   this trampling of my courts?
> Bring no more vain offerings."
>   (Isaiah 1:11-13)

Other Old Testament passages express a similar principle: God wants people to serve him with clean hands and clean hearts. He wants people who are morally upright, people who seek justice and oppose oppression, people who have compassion for the poor and the fatherless. Outward ceremonial displays, such as animal sacrifices offered without a repentant and righteous heart, are worthless and offensive to God (see also Jeremiah 7:22, Hosea 5:6, and Psalm 51:16).

These injustices made Jesus angry. To say he was "righteously indignant" is to downplay and diminish both his anger and the cause of his anger. It is especially offensive to God when evil men oppress the innocent and the poor while invoking God's name. Such intense evil ought to offend us as well. If we can look upon such evil and not feel angry, then something is wrong with us.

Jesus was angry. Call it righteous anger if you must, but let's not dismiss it as mere indignation.

The Healthy Anger of Jesus

Another incident in the life of Jesus clearly demonstrates his ability to be righteously angry. In Mark 3, Jesus entered a synagogue on the Sabbath day and saw a man with a withered hand. The religious leaders stood by, watching Jesus to see if he would heal the man. They hoped to catch him in the act of doing work on the Sabbath so they could condemn him under their interpretation of the Law.

Jesus called the man with a withered hand to come to him, and then he asked the religious leaders, "Is it lawful on the Sabbath to do good or to do harm, to save life or to kill?" There was an uncomfortable silence in the room; none of the religious leaders dared answer. Mark records that Jesus "looked around at them with anger, grieved at their hardness of heart." Then he said to the man, "Stretch out your hand." The man did so—and his hand was fully restored. Enraged, the religious leaders went out and plotted to kill Jesus (see Mark 3:1-6).

Isn't that ironic? Jesus asked them if it was lawful to do good on the Sabbath or to kill? They refused to answer his question. And when Jesus healed the man, they went out to plot murder on the Sabbath! Who, then, were the real Sabbath-breakers in this account?

As we look at these two instances of anger in the life of Jesus, we do not see the slightest hint that God was displeased with the anger of his Son. Nowhere in the Bible does God ever tell us we must never be angry. It's a sin to lash out in anger and hurt other people. It's a sin to hate, to nurse grudges, to stubbornly remain bitter, resentful, and unforgiving. But anger is not the same as these sins. Anger toward sin and injustice is part of the holy character of God.

The Old Testament contains many references to God's anger: Deuteronomy 1:37; 4:21; 9:8,20; 1 Kings 8:46; Psalm 2:12; 79:5; 85:5; and Isaiah 12:1. The apostle Paul makes a clear distinction between anger and sin in Ephesians 4:26: "Be angry and do not sin; do not let the sun go down on your anger."

In 1 Timothy 3 and Titus 1, Paul talks about the qualifications for an overseer (that is, a bishop or leader in the church), and he says that an overseer must be self-controlled, not violent, not quarrelsome, and not quick-tempered. In other words, a leader should be a person who is slow to anger, who keeps his anger under control, and who does not let his anger lead him to sin.

As a friend once told me, "Only two kinds of people never get angry—the physically dead and the emotionally dead." Anger is a normal emotion that people experience from time to time. Those who follow the leadership style of Jesus will

- direct their anger only toward the things that anger God, such as sin and injustice
- keep their anger under control and not let anger control them
- not use anger as an excuse to hurt others with harmful actions or cruel remarks
- not let anger turn to bitterness and hate

Christlike leaders will sometimes be angry, but it will be the right kind of anger. Healthy, Christlike anger can be a great weapon against injustice and evil.

On May 3, 1980, thirteen-year-old Cari Lightner was killed by a hit-and-run driver while walking to a church carnival in Fair Oaks,

California. The driver was drunk, was out on bail from another drunk driving hit-and-run, and had been arrested for drunk driving five times in four years. The police told Cari's mother, Candy Lightner, that the man who had killed her daughter would probably not do any jail time at all.

In the midst of her grief, Candy Lightner was angry. The legal system was not protecting people against deadly drunk drivers. If it were protecting the public, her daughter would still be alive. The evening of Cari's funeral, Candy Lightner announced that she was going to start an organization to make a difference and save lives. That organization, appropriately enough, became known as Mothers Against Drunk Driving—MADD.

Candy Lightner is a leader who practices the leadership style of Jesus. Injustice made her angry, and she channeled her anger into a solution for that injustice. MADD promoted stricter laws, stiffer penalties, tougher enforcement, victims' advocacy in the criminal justice system, victim support and counseling, alcohol education, creative ideas such as "designated drivers" and alternative transportation, and more.

Righteous anger has motivated many important reform movements over the years, including the abolition movement to end slavery, the civil rights movement, the anti-drug-abuse movement, and efforts to end child abuse, child neglect, and child pornography. That's the proper use of anger—to fight injustice, protect the innocent, and solve problems.

As John Wesley once said, "Give me a hundred men who fear nothing but God, and who hate nothing but sin, and who know nothing but Jesus Christ and him crucified, and I will shake the world." So be angry over the things that anger God, let that anger motivate you, and go out and shake the world.

The Danger of Unhealthy Anger

Are you satisfied with the way you handle your anger? Are you volatile or explosive by nature? Do you need to learn to control your anger? A leadership role tends to expose us to stressful situations. If we are unable to handle stress, conflict, obstacles, opposition, and crises with a cool and calm demeanor, if we tend to blow up under pressure, that trait will undermine our leadership performance. The person who cannot control his or her temper cannot lead like Jesus.

The first step in managing our anger is *to accept personal responsibility for our emotions.* We have to stop making excuses for our lack of self-control. You've undoubtedly heard some of these excuses, and you may have even made them yourself:

- "I'm a redhead, and all redheads lose their temper quickly."
- "I'm Italian (or Spanish or Middle Eastern or whatever), and we're a hot-blooded people."
- "I come from a family where anger is normal."
- "I've heard it's unhealthy to bottle up your emotions, so I express my emotions all the time."
- "I like to let people know where I stand. That's just who I am. If you don't like it, that's your problem."

These are just rationalizations for emotional immaturity and lack of self-control. Leaders, especially Christlike leaders, need to set an example of character growth and self-discipline. As a leader, do you really want to communicate to the people you lead that you are unable to govern your emotions and your behavior? If anger is your Achilles' heel, consider getting counseling and learning strategies for controlling your emotions in times of stress and opposition. Having dealt with this issue in my life, I can testify that God can deliver you from it if you are ready for God to do his work in you.

The second step in managing our anger is *to understand what anger does to us.* Anger causes physiological changes in the body because our bodies are actually preparing us for a fight. Adrenaline is pumped into the bloodstream. Blood pressure increases. The heart beats faster. Blood even clots more quickly than normal as the body prepares for possible injury. The pupils of our eyes dilate, our muscles tense, and the digestive tract can sometimes spasm, causing abdominal pain.

Anger mobilizes us for action. But because the causes of our anger seldom require a fistfight, much of that tension ends up being bottled up inside us. As a result, those angry emotions often lead to long-term physical and psychological problems, including heart disease, high blood pressure, heart attack and stroke, depression, and more. Many people think that by unleashing their anger and lashing out at people, they are somehow ridding themselves of anger, but in reality giving way to angry emotions often causes anger to escalate. So we are doing ourselves no favor by getting mad.

The third step in managing our anger is *to study the example of Jesus*. We should examine the anger of Jesus in detail. If we look at his cleansing of the temple and his confrontation with the religious leaders over the man with the withered hand, we will see that Jesus always controlled his anger. He directed it against hypocrisy and injustice. He used his anger to solve problems, such as the pollution of God's house by the money changers, merchants, and corrupt priests.

The anger of Jesus was always focused on sin and injustice. When angered, Jesus didn't lash out at everyone in sight. His anger did not create collateral damage or do harm to innocent victims. Those who felt the heat of his anger clearly deserved to be chastised. Jesus didn't simply blow off steam. He used his anger to achieve justice. Our anger needs to be as righteous, controlled, and focused as his was.

The fourth step in managing our anger is *to make sure that we direct our anger at problems, not people*. The old saying applies: "Hate the sin, but love the sinner." Righteous anger always attacks evil, sin, corruption, oppression, and injustice, but it also seeks to redeem and reform the sinner. Our goal should never be revenge or attack. It should always be redemption and restoration.

This brings us to our next leadership principle:

Principle 12

Like Jesus,
authentic leaders express anger in healthy ways.

Part 4

The
Problems
of Leadership

13

The
Lonely Calling

If you considered running for political office, one of the first steps you would take is to find out how much public support your candidacy might receive. Would the voters be receptive to your message? Would there be a strong donor base to provide financial support? Would your political party back you with funding, media support, and advisers?

If you wanted to open a new business, some of the first questions you'd ask yourself might be: Is there a market for your product or service? How strong and aggressive is the competition? Do you have enough capital available to get you through the startup period?

If you wanted to plant a new church, you would need to ask yourself: Are there enough people in the area to support a new church? Who are we trying to reach (what is our target demographic)? Does the area need a new church or is it already overserved with churches? What should the distinctive mission of this church be? How will the church be funded and supported during the startup period?

When I decided to write this book, I had to answer two questions (not only for my own information, but because I knew a good publisher would ask them anyway): First, who is the target audience for this book? Second, are there enough people in that audience to make this book worthy of a publisher's effort and resources?

Before a leader launches any new venture, he or she needs to ask some probing questions, do the necessary research, and face the answers to those questions unflinchingly and realistically. Jesus expressed this principle in Luke 14: "For which of you, desiring to build a tower, does not first sit down and count the cost, whether he has enough to complete it?" (verse 28). Though Jesus was talking about the cost of discipleship, not the cost of starting a business or church, the principle applies.

Yet, even though you have done all the research, conducted all the studies, and analyzed all the facts and figures, the venture can still fail. The political race can end in defeat. The startup business can end in bankruptcy. The new church may close its doors. The book may fail to find its audience.

What do you do when it turns out that the support you hoped for is not there? What do you do if your best-laid plans go awry and you find you are a leader without followers?

A Leader Without Followers?

In the early days of the Lord's earthly ministry, no one would have foreseen that this lone Galilean preacher was launching a global spiritual movement that would span at least two thousand years of history. In fact, marketing experts and public relations strategists might have concluded that he was going about it all wrong.

First, *Jesus targeted the wrong demographic group*. He should have pitched his message at the upper classes of Jewish society, where all the influence, power, and money were concentrated. Instead, he wasted his time and effort preaching to the poor, the sick, the despised tax collectors, the political zealots—the very dregs of society.

Second, *Jesus alienated the rich and powerful*. It wasn't bad enough that he pitched his message to the poor and powerless, but he actually went out of his way to stir up conflict with the top echelon of society. The Pharisees and Sadducees and priests could have been influential patrons of his cause if he had just sidled up to them, flattered them, and tried to win them over as friends and allies.

Third, *Jesus was a poor salesman.* Successful salespeople know how to highlight the benefits of the product, overcome objections, sweeten the offer, and close the sale. Jesus had a tendency to highlight the costs, provoke objections, and remind people of the drawbacks to following him. He said, "Whoever does not bear his own cross and come after me cannot be my disciple" (Luke 14:27). And, "If your right eye causes you to sin, tear it out and throw it away" (Matthew 5:29). And, "Go, sell all that you have and give to the poor" (Mark 10:21). Any good salesman would tell you that Jesus will never close the sale with a sales pitch like those.

Fourth, *Jesus was uncompromising.* He didn't seem to know how the game is played. You have to go along to get along. Sometimes you have to compromise your principles to get closer to your goal. One hand washes the other, you know.

At times it seemed that Jesus didn't really care if anyone supported his cause or not. Near the end of John 6, there's a scene where Jesus, while teaching in the synagogue at Capernaum, talks about being the bread of life that comes down from heaven. He even says, "Whoever feeds on my flesh and drinks my blood has eternal life" (John 6:54a). Hearing this, many of the people who had been following him were scandalized. They said, "This is a hard saying; who can listen to it?" At that point, many of those who had been his disciples turned away and refused to follow him.

After the other disciples left, Jesus turned to the Twelve and said, "Do you want to go away as well?" (John 6:67).

Simon Peter replied, "Lord, to whom shall we go? You have the words of eternal life, and we have believed, and have come to know, that you are the Holy One of God" (John 6:68-69).

The Twelve remained. But what if they had abandoned him? What if Jesus had been left all alone, a leader without any followers? I believe that Jesus, though saddened, would have carried on his ministry. He had come in obedience to save the human race, with or without the support of the people. He would do what he came to do.

Guidelines for Lonely Leaders

Some years ago, a Christian man had an idea that he thought was the perfect combination of capitalism and evangelism. He would help fellow Christians earn money while spreading the gospel at the same time. His plan was to create a line of products imprinted with Scripture verses and inspirational sayings. He contacted friends and acquaintances and offered to let them invest in his concept for a thousand dollars per investor.

When he explained the concept to potential investors, he produced graphs and charts that showed how investors could expect to make at least 18 percent on their investment during the first two years. He planned to sell more stock in his venture and distribute his wares all over the United States and Canada, and even overseas. Almost instantly, he lined up fifty enthusiastic backers.

One day, he received a notice from the Securities and Exchange Commission, telling him that he had violated the law by the manner in which he had issued stock in his venture. But the man ignored the notice from the government and he continued issuing stock. "The government is just trying to interfere with the gospel," he said.

A few weeks passed, and the notices from the government became more stern and threatening. Finally, the government charged him with violations of federal law. As a result, his business was shut down and his backers lost every cent they had invested.

"As soon as you try to do something great for the Lord," the man said, "Satan puts up a fight." I think it's more likely that this man brought his troubles on himself by flouting the law. He had the enthusiastic support of fifty investors, but he squandered it by refusing to play by the rules.

When Jesus lost the support of his followers (all but the Twelve), he didn't do anything wrong. His followers deserted him because they finally realized what he was actually saying to them, and they couldn't handle the truth. Many of the early followers of Jesus had projected onto him their own political and social hopes and dreams.

They thought he came as a revolutionary and a liberator who would throw off the yoke of Roman oppression and return the nation of Israel to its former glory.

The more Jesus taught about the spiritual nature of his kingdom and his messiahship, the more people became disillusioned and disenchanted. They realized that Jesus was not the kind of king they thought he would be—and not the kind of king they wanted. They didn't abandon Jesus because he wasn't a good marketing strategist or a good salesman. They didn't abandon Jesus because there was anything wrong with his message. They abandoned him because the truth is hard for most people to take.

As you and I seek to live out the leadership style of Jesus, there will be times when we speak the truth and the truth will cost us followers. The truth will cost us sales and profits. The truth may even cost us our leadership position. If we have to pay a price for speaking the truth, then so be it. We are simply following in the footsteps of the Master, who paid the ultimate price on the cross.

But if we, as leaders, are going to pay a price, let's make sure it is for the right reasons. Let's make sure that we are truly paying a price for defending God's truth, not for behaving foolishly like the man who ignored the government's warnings. Let's make sure that we are truly being persecuted for the truth and not disgracing God's truth with our own foolish actions.

In our human imperfection and pride, we often confuse our agenda with God's agenda. We easily assume that when we suffer opposition, we are being persecuted for our faith. Unlike Jesus, we are fallible. Our motives, at best, are mixed and unreliable. When we listen for God's voice, our sin nature sometimes affects our hearing. Here are some suggestions for learning to hear God's voice more clearly:

1. Continually search your motives. We need to check our plans against God's Word and make sure that we are obedient to his will for our lives. We need to take an honest look within and ask ourselves:

Am I living obediently for God? Or am I only serving my own ego? Am I serving God's will? Or am I being self-willed and stubborn? Am I being honest with myself? Or am I deceiving myself?

2. *Continually seek guidance from God.* We need to prayerfully ask God to reveal to us the hidden reasons why we do the things we do. We need to remember that prayer is a two-way conversation with God. There is a time for speaking—and a time for listening. "Be still," the Lord says, "and know that I am God" (Psalm 46:10a).

3. *Be accountable to some trusted Christian friends.* We all need a circle of close friends who meet with us regularly, who pray for us and hold us accountable, and who care enough about us to tell us the truth about ourselves, including the truth we don't want to hear. Every leader needs a few close friends he or she can confide in, and who will provide a regular and much-needed reality check.

Do you have friends like that in your leadership life? Leadership is often a lonely calling. We all need the support of a few close friends to keep us honest, energized, motivated, and on the right track.

Never Alone at the Top

I know of a couple who felt God calling them to be missionaries in Africa. The country God had laid on their hearts was going through a time of revolution, violence, and widespread terrorism. Their families and friends tried to dissuade them from going, especially since this couple had three preschool-age children. The mission board also advised against their plans.

Yet this couple told their prayer-support group, "We have such an inner assurance from God that it doesn't matter if no one supports us. We know that God is with us and we are determined to go."

So they went—and they spent several years having an effective outreach for God in that troubled country. Had they listened to the opposing voices of family, friends, and the mission board, they never would have gone.

We see a similar situation in the life of the apostle Paul. During Paul's third and final missionary journey, he spent almost three years in Ephesus, teaching and organizing missionary activity in the region. At the end of his stay in Ephesus, Paul felt the Holy Spirit urging him to go to Jerusalem and then on to Rome (see Acts 19:21). When Paul came under attack from the silversmiths who produced the pagan idols in Ephesus, he left the city and journeyed through Greece, Macedonia, and Anatolia.

Stopping in Miletus in Anatolia, Paul sent to Ephesus for the elders of the church to meet with him. At the meeting, Paul told the elders he was going to Jerusalem. The elders wept over Paul and embraced him, because they knew he was a wanted man and would be arrested if he went to Jerusalem (see Acts 20:17-38).

From Miletus, Paul sailed to Caesarea (with several stops in between), and there he and his companions stayed in the home of Philip the evangelist. During their stay, they were visited by a Christian prophet named Agabus. This prophet took Paul's belt, bound his own hands and feet with it, then prophesied, "Thus says the Holy Spirit, 'This is how the Jews at Jerusalem will bind the man who owns this belt and deliver him into the hands of the Gentiles.'" Hearing this prophecy, Paul's friends urged him not to go to Jerusalem.

"What are you doing, weeping and breaking my heart?" Paul said. "For I am ready not only to be imprisoned but even to die in Jerusalem for the name of the Lord Jesus."

Paul's friends could not persuade him, so they said, "Let the will of the Lord be done" (see Acts 21:1-14).

The prophecy of Agabus was fulfilled. Paul went to Jerusalem, where he became embroiled in a conflict that led to his arrest and imprisonment. He was imprisoned by the Romans for a while in Caesarea, and then he was taken in chains to Rome.

Some Christians read this account and criticize Paul for not listening to Agabus and the other Christians who warned him to stay away from Jerusalem. But the book of Acts tells us plainly that "Paul resolved in the Spirit to...go to Jerusalem, saying, 'After I have been there, I must also see Rome'" (Acts 19:21). Paul knew what awaited him in Jerusalem, but he went in obedience to the leading of the Holy Spirit.

Sometimes a leader must stand alone. Paul was not *totally* alone, of course, because the Spirit of God was with him. But all of Paul's friends were opposed to his plans. They were concerned for his life, and rightly so. But God sometimes tells a leader to go places and do things that defy human reason. Paul knew that God had a purpose for sending him to Jerusalem and then to Rome. Paul knew that God wanted him to go to Rome as his ambassador, even as an ambassador in chains.

As leaders following the leadership style of Jesus, at times we may feel called by God to go in a specific direction—a direction that defies all the counsel we received from Christian friends and advisers. Before we commit ourselves to such a course, we need to take every precaution to make sure we are certain of God's will. We need to make sure we are acting out of conviction and obedience, not stubbornness and self-will.

But once we know that God is calling us to a certain course of action, we must do it, even if no one else agrees. We must stand alone, with no support but God's.

The psalmist wrote, "For my father and my mother have forsaken me, but the LORD will take me in" (Psalm 27:10). No one feels more lonely and abandoned than that. On the cross, Jesus knew what it meant to be completely alone, a leader without followers, forsaken even by his Father. The Twelve had abandoned him, and one had even betrayed him. Just before his death, he cried out, "My God, my God, why have you forsaken me?" (Mark 15:34).

If you ever feel lonely in leadership, remember Jesus on the cross—the loneliest, most abandoned, most rejected leader in the history of the world. There's a saying that "it's lonely at the top." No one knew that truth better than Jesus. Yet this same Jesus has promised never to leave you or forsake you.

So the next time you feel alone and unsupported, and the weight of your leadership role is pressing down on you, remember there is Someone with you who understands. Jesus is with you, and you are never alone.

The Loneliness of Command

"Command is lonely," Colin Powell wrote in *My American Journey*.[1] No one understood the loneliness of command better than General Dwight D. Eisenhower.

At 4:00 a.m. on June 5, 1944, General Eisenhower conferred with his staff on the loneliest and most momentous decision of his military career—the decision whether to launch Operation Overlord, the D-Day assault, the first step toward liberating Western Europe from Nazi Germany. A force of 4,400 ships, 11,000 planes, and nearly 155,000 troops awaited the decision that only he could make—a decision to send them across the English Channel to the French shores. Weather had already postponed the invasion for at least twenty-four hours. Because of the tides, a decision to postpone would put the invasion back for at least two more weeks.

The success of Operation Overlord depended on the weather. A predicted break in the storm would give the allies a chance to catch the Nazi forces by surprise. But weather prediction was an iffy business in those days, and a mistaken prediction could prove disastrous.

One of Eisenhower's commanders, British Admiral Bertram Ramsay, reminded him that the ships were already in the channel in rough seas. The decision to either go or abort would have to be transmitted to the fleet within the next thirty minutes. As the storm howled outside the headquarters, Eisenhower took a poll of his commanders—go or abort? They were evenly divided.

The decision was Eisenhower's alone. One of the commanders in that room, General Walter Bedell Smith, later recalled those tense

moments as General Eisenhower sat quietly and pondered his decision. Smith said that Eisenhower was silent for at least five full minutes, lost in thought. "I never realized before," Smith reflected, "the
loneliness and isolation of a commander at a time when such a
momentous decision has to be taken, with the full knowledge that
failure or success rests on his judgment alone."[2]

Finally, Eisenhower spoke. "Okay, we'll go," he said. With those
three words, he launched the largest military operation that had ever
been attempted. At that moment, the liberation of Europe began.

Earlier that day, General Eisenhower had handwritten a note on
a plain sheet of notepaper, which he had folded and tucked into his
wallet. It was a message he hoped he would never have to deliver,
and it was proof of the loneliness that is so often a part of any leadership position. He wrote:

> Our landings in the Cherbourg-Havre area have failed
> to gain a satisfactory foothold and I have withdrawn the
> troops. My decision to attack at this time and place was
> based upon the best information available. The troops,
> the air and the Navy did all that Bravery and devotion
> to duty could do. If any blame or fault attaches to the
> attempt it is mine alone.—June 5.[3]

That note was an admission of defeat—and it never had to be
delivered. Though the hard-fought D-Day attack cost many lives,
it was successful. It was the beginning of the end of World War II.

Leadership is a lonely calling, and we as leaders are often required
to make hard decisions in which the blame or fault is ours alone. We
can gather around us a circle of supporters, people who will pray
for us and advise us and support us during those moments of lonely
decision. But leaders must ultimately make the lonely decisions.

If everyone turns away and forsakes us, if no one will stand by
our side, we still have a friend. Jesus the Master has walked that

lonely leadership road. He knows the way, and he will never leave us or forsake us.

That is why our next leadership principle is:

Principle 13

One authentic leader plus Jesus the Lord
equals a strong majority.

14   Doubters

Jesus demonstrated his leadership ability by taking people from a variety of backgrounds and molding them into a unified community focused on a single goal—the Great Commission goal of evangelizing the world. Jesus displayed this remarkable ability when he called the twelve apostles—several working-class stiffs (Peter, Andrew, James, and John), a political agitator (Simon the Zealot), a social outcast (Matthew the tax collector), and more. As someone once said of the Twelve, "There wasn't one impressive résumé in the lot."

Even after his resurrection, Jesus demonstrated his leadership ability, still molding and shaping the nucleus of his new kingdom community, still teaching and mentoring and leading his followers. The first person Jesus appeared to after his resurrection was Mary Magdalene, the most loyal of all his followers. She stood at the foot of the cross as he died and was the first to reach the empty tomb on the morning he arose. In that first-century culture, women were not permitted to be witnesses in legal proceedings, so when Jesus made Mary Magdalene the first witness to the resurrection, he elevated and affirmed the status of all women.

He reached out in a special way to Peter, the once-proud and blustery disciple, the one who swore he would never forsake Jesus—then, during the crisis of the Lord's trial, swore he'd never met Jesus. After the resurrection, Peter was repentant but filled with shame and self-reproach because of his cowardice and defection. Jesus elevated and affirmed Peter and restored him to a position of leadership in the newly founded church.

Jesus also reached out to two disciples who were walking to the village of Emmaus, about seven miles northwest of Jerusalem. One of the disciples was named Cleopas while the other is unnamed in Luke 24. It was the day of the Lord's resurrection, and the two disciples were discussing the news that the tomb had been found empty that morning. As they talked, a stranger asked them what they were discussing. The stranger reminded them of the prophecies about the Messiah, and later, as the two disciples and the stranger sat down for a meal together, the disciples suddenly recognized him as the resurrected Lord—and he vanished from their sight.

"Did not our hearts burn within us," they said, "while he talked to us on the road, while he opened to us the Scriptures?" And they went and told the rest of the disciples (see Luke 24:13-35).

This was Jesus the Master, the quintessential leader, teaching, mentoring, encouraging, comforting, blessing, and preparing his followers. But of all the disciples Jesus reached out to after his resurrection, the toughest challenge to his leadership skills was probably the apostle Thomas, also known as Didymus ("the twin"). History remembers Thomas the apostle by his nickname "Doubting Thomas," because of the incident recorded in John 20:24-29.

Thomas was not present when Jesus appeared to the disciples, so he had seemingly missed his chance to see the risen Lord. Eight days later, Thomas and the disciples were together again and the others told him, "We have seen the Lord." But Thomas wouldn't believe them. "Unless I see in his hands the marks of the nails," Thomas said, "and place my finger into the mark of the nails, and place my hand into his side, I will never believe."

For more than a week, Thomas remained an unbeliever. In effect, he was calling his fellow disciples liars. He set an unreasonably high standard of proof.

But eight days after the resurrection, as Thomas and the other disciples were again gathered in a room behind locked doors, Jesus appeared to them, stood among them, and invited Thomas to put out his hand and touch the evidence. Only then was Thomas convinced. He replied, "My Lord and my God!"

Holy Skepticism Versus Unholy Doubt

Why was Thomas so skeptical? His tendency toward unbelief was undoubtedly rooted in his habitual pessimism.

Earlier in John's gospel Jesus told the disciples that he was going to the village of Bethany following the death of Lazarus. When Thomas heard this, he told his fellow disciples, "Let us also go, that we may die with him" (John 11:16). Though Thomas was certainly loyal to the Lord, his outlook was cynical and fatalistic.

Leaders are often called upon to deal with doubters like Thomas—managers, employees, team members, soldiers, church members, or family members who have a pessimistic mindset, who do not believe in the leader's vision and goals, who do not expect success or victory, who are skeptical and doubtful and generally gloomy. Like Thomas, many of these people have preconceived ideas and are unwilling to change. They are wary and unwilling to trust, and they demand proof of anything you say.

I'm not saying that we should expect our followers to be gullible and unquestioning. It's wise to maintain a certain level of holy skepticism, the ability to discern truth from lies, the genuine from the counterfeit, so that we won't be taken in by deceivers and con men. That's why the apostle John wrote, "Beloved, do not believe every spirit, but test the spirits to see whether they are from God, for many false prophets have gone out into the world" (1 John 4:1).

But the apostle Thomas took skepticism too far. He had heard the testimony of Mary Magdalene, Peter, James, John, Cleopas, and the other disciples—and he had written it all off as a pack of lies (or at best, mass delusion). Eyewitness testimony is considered valid in every court of law, yet Thomas refused to accept the testimony of many witnesses. He refused to believe in the resurrection unless he could literally probe the Lord's wounds with his fingers.

The stubborn, hard-nosed, inconvincible doubter is a challenge to every person in leadership. Pessimistic doubters often sow discord, discontent, suspicion, and division in an organization. Doubters turn conversations into arguments. They put a suspicious or pessimistic twist on every word you speak. The Arabs have a saying: "Your beloved will swallow gravel for you, but your enemy will count your every error." A doubter can quickly become your enemy, spreading division among your followers, dampening enthusiasm and morale, and calling your vision and goals into question.

Stubborn, pessimistic doubt is at the root of division and strife in countless organizations, teams, churches, and homes. Just as doubts about God make people unwilling to submit to his authority, doubts about leaders undermine their leadership authority. It is vitally important that leaders recognize and deal with the problem of doubters in the organization.

How did Jesus deal with Thomas, his doubting follower? To answer that question, let's examine the Lord's response to Thomas within the context of his leadership style.

Evidence Is Not the Problem

It's significant that Jesus waited eight days before appearing the second time to the disciples. Why did Jesus wait? Wouldn't it have been kinder to Thomas and the others if he had appeared to them again within a few hours or days? Instead, he left the disciples alone to think about what they had witnessed, to ponder what it meant. He gave Thomas time to stew in his own doubt and unbelief. He gave them all time to recall all the things he had said when he was among them, teaching and mentoring them.

During those eight days, the disciples had time to reflect on the past and the future. Some may have had moments when they questioned their own sanity, but the evidence was overwhelming. All but Thomas had seen the Lord with their own eyes. Mary Magdalene had spoken with Jesus at the tomb. Cleopas and the other disciple had spoken with the risen Lord on the road to Emmaus, and he had taught them about himself from the Old Testament prophecies. They needed time to discuss all that they had witnessed and all that they had learned.

If you are a parent, then you remember when your toddlers were learning to walk. You stood a few feet back, encouraging your child to take those first steps. You remained close enough to protect your child, but far enough away to encourage your child to gain confidence and launch out on his own.

I believe that Jesus was leading his followers in much the same way. I suspect he was close by, observing and listening to everything they said. Perhaps he was among them but unrecognized, just as he was unrecognized on the road to Emmaus. In any case, I believe he was close enough to protect them, but far enough away to allow them to gain confidence and build their faith.

Finally, after eight days, Jesus returned and stood among them. This time, he did not concern himself so much with the entire group. Instead, he singled out the doubter, the one who had demanded proof under laboratory conditions.

In his approach to Thomas, Jesus didn't do what leaders so often do today. He did not speak to the entire group, giving a generalized speech on the problem of doubt, hoping that the one doubter would get the message. Nor did Jesus surround himself with yes-men, excluding the doubters and hoping they would get the message and leave.

As a leader, Jesus leaned toward the direct approach. His solution was to concentrate on the doubter—not to shame him or humiliate him in front of his peers but to address his doubts and questions openly, for all to see. Even though Thomas's demand for proof was unreasonable and excessive, Jesus met the demand. He presented exactly the proof Thomas said he had to have in order to believe.

Put yourself in the sandals of Doubting Thomas. Can you imagine the shame, embarrassment, and brokenness Thomas must have felt when Jesus recited Thomas's words back to him? Eight days earlier, Thomas had said, "Unless I see in his hands the mark of the nails, and place my finger into the mark of the nails, and place my hand into his side, I will never believe." Now Jesus says to him, "Put your finger here, and see my hands; and put out your hand, and place it in my side. Do not disbelieve, but believe."

There is no surer way to make a person ashamed of his foolish words than to repeat them back to him later. Often, the most stinging rebuke a leader can make to a doubting follower is to simply give him the proof he demands.

John's account does not say that Thomas actually inspected the evidence as he said he would. There is no indication that Thomas actually felt the Lord's wounds with his own hands, even though Jesus invited him to do so. All we know is that Thomas was utterly convinced, and he cried out, "My Lord and my God!"

The way the Lord dealt with Doubting Thomas is a masterful blend of toughness and tenderness, rebuke and restoration. After inviting Thomas to inspect the physical evidence, and after Thomas responded by expressing his belief, Jesus said, "Have you believed because you have seen me? Blessed are those who have not seen and yet have believed" (see John 20:24-29).

The Lord Jesus accepted the belated faith of Doubting Thomas and offered him reconciliation and restoration. But Jesus also rebuked his earlier unbelief. He warned, "Do not disbelieve, but believe."

Jesus was saying to Thomas, and to all of us, that when doubters doubt, it's not because the evidence is lacking. It's because something is lacking within the doubter. Thomas had plenty of evidence all along. The testimony of the other disciples should have convinced him. But the gloomy, pessimistic nature of Thomas predisposed him to unbelief.

This is an important principle to remember in your leadership experience: When a habitual doubter questions your leadership, your vision, your goals, or your agenda, his problem may not be a lack of evidence. His problem may be his own pessimistic and distrustful disposition.

From Doubt to Faith

The leadership style of Jesus was not task-focused but people-focused. As a leader, Jesus didn't merely want to achieve goals and objectives. He was continually moving people from immaturity to maturity, from doubt to faith, from skepticism to commitment, from enmity to love. When Jesus had to confront his followers, he didn't do so to shame them or humiliate them. He was continually helping them grow toward their God-given potential.

Clearly, the leadership strategy of Jesus accomplished its goal. In an instant, the skepticism of Thomas was transformed to faith and commitment. Thomas was a changed man. From then on, his mission was to reach others with the good news of Jesus Christ. I imagine he had a special ministry among doubters and skeptics because he understood how they thought.

When Jesus called his disciples and assembled this diverse group of followers known as the Twelve, he knew what kind of follower Thomas would be. He knew what a challenge this pessimistic doubter would pose to his leadership ability. And he wanted Thomas on his team for a special purpose. Thomas was the Lord's choice to be his select apostle to doubters and skeptics, to pessimists and cynics.

These insights bring us to our next leadership principle:

Principle 14

Authentic leaders turn doubters into believers.

15   Criticism

I once saw this sign on the desk of an executive: "To avoid criticism: Say nothing. Do nothing. Be nothing." Of course, anyone who says nothing and does nothing is, by definition, *not* a leader. To be a leader is to be a target for criticism.

Theodore Roosevelt understood it is the leader in the arena, not the critic, who actually impacts events and changes the course of history. At a speech in Paris a year after he left the White House, Roosevelt said:

> It is not the critic who counts; not the man who points
> out how the strong man stumbles, or where the doer of
> deeds could have done better. The credit belongs to the
> man in the arena, whose face is marred by dust and sweat
> and blood, who strives valiantly...who knows the great
> enthusiasms, the great devotions, who spends himself
> for a worthy cause; who, at the best knows in the end
> the triumph of high achievement, and who at the worst,
> if he fails, at least he fails while daring greatly, so that his
> place shall never be with those cold and timid souls who
> knew neither victory nor defeat. [1]

The world has been changed and history has been made by leaders, not critics. It's the one in the arena who counts.

No one is immune to criticism. The most admired and revered leaders in history have all been subject to harsh and unfair criticism.

George Washington, America's first (and perhaps greatest) president, is widely regarded as a man of impeccable honor and character. Yet Thomas Paine, another founding father and a former friend to Washington, once wrote a scathing open letter to Washington that included these words: "And as to you, sir, treacherous in private friendship…and a hypocrite in public life, the world will be puzzled to decide whether you are an apostate or an impostor; whether you have abandoned good principles, or whether you ever had any." [2]

Another great leader who endured intense criticism was Abraham Lincoln. One of Lincoln's most bitter critics was attorney Edwin Stanton. Lincoln and Stanton became acquainted in 1857 when they both served on the same legal team in a lawsuit. For some reason, Stanton despised Lincoln and publicly mocked him, calling him "a low, cunning clown," "the original gorilla," and a man afflicted with "painful imbecility."

In 1861, Lincoln was inaugurated as the sixteenth president of the United States, and the following year he appointed Stanton as secretary of war, a crucial post during the Civil War. Lincoln knew that Stanton despised him—but Lincoln also knew that Stanton was honest and dependable. The war was going badly, largely because of bureaucratic incompetence in the War Department, but Lincoln knew that Stanton would make the War Department work like a well-oiled machine.

After Stanton joined the cabinet, Lincoln would walk to the War Office every day and confer with Stanton as battlefield reports came in over the telegraph. In time, Stanton began to appreciate the wisdom, intelligence, and sincerity of the president. The two adversaries became allies—and in time, they became friends. When the news came of the surrender of the Confederacy, the two men actually embraced.

On April 14, 1865, when Lincoln succumbed to an assassin's bullet, Edwin Stanton was grief-stricken. Lincoln's eldest son, Robert Todd Lincoln, was twenty-one when his father died, and he recalled that for days after Lincoln's death, Stanton would come to Robert's room every morning and sit with him, weeping without saying a word.

Every leader endures criticism. Sometimes, as was the case with Abraham Lincoln, a leader can turn his critics into friends.

Unfortunately, however, that's not always possible.

The Critics of Jesus

Jesus was opposed by critics throughout his ministry. His opponents hated him for many reasons, including jealousy over his popularity and resentment of his power to heal diseases and restore sight to the blind. Out of their bitterness, they said, "You have a demon" (see John 7:20). Today's secular critics would probably say, "You are mentally ill and ought to be locked up."

The Lord's opponents had no just cause for hating him. All their reasons for hating Jesus were unjust, selfish, and sinful. They hated him because of his good deeds and his righteous message. As Jesus himself said, "Whoever hates me hates my Father also. If I had not done among them the works that no one else did, they would not be guilty of sin, but now they have seen and hated both me and my Father. But the word that is written in their Law must be fulfilled: 'They hated me without a cause'" (John 15:23-25).

I have always wondered how people could see the evidence of the life of Jesus, his healing power and his compassion for suffering people, and still speak against him. But they did. When Jesus healed the man by the pool at Bethesda, the religious leaders didn't rejoice. They attacked Jesus for healing on the Sabbath. In fact, that was one of several times that they plotted to murder Jesus (see John 5:1-16).

On another Sabbath day, Jesus healed a man who had been born blind. Some of the Pharisees grumbled, "This man is not from God, for he does not keep the Sabbath." They complained that Jesus wouldn't obey all of their legalistic rules and regulations. But some of the Pharisees paused to wonder, "How can a man who is a sinner do such signs?" As a result, there was division and conflict among the Pharisees over Jesus.

Ultimately, hatred overcame reason. The religious leaders arrested Jesus and hauled him before Pontius Pilate, the Roman governor. When Pilate asked what Jesus had been charged with, they replied, "If this man were not doing evil, we would not have delivered him over to you" (John 18:30).

Isn't it strange that the enemies of Jesus couldn't list his specific crimes? And Pilate clearly saw that the Lord's enemies were railroading him, because he replied, "Take him yourselves and judge him by your own law." Pilate knew the religious leaders were scheming to get the Romans to do their dirty work, and he wanted no part of it.

But the religious leaders felt entitled to get their way. They were the cultural aristocracy in Israel, and if they said Jesus deserved punishment and death, then Pontius Pilate should take their word for it. The critics of Jesus were so powerful and influential that even Pontius Pilate, the representative of the oppressive Roman occupation, was intimidated by them. They expected Pilate to do their bidding—and he did.

The enemies of Jesus continued trying to stamp out the Christian faith for years after the death and resurrection of Christ. Near the end of the book of Acts, the early church was established throughout Palestine and across Asia Minor and up into Greece and Macedonia. The apostle Paul, having finally reached Rome, met with the Jewish religious leaders there to talk to them about Jesus.

The Jewish leaders in Rome agreed to hear what Paul had to say, but some were already skeptical of his message, saying, "For with regard to this sect [Christianity] we know that everywhere it is spoken against" (Acts 28:22). So Paul taught them about Jesus from the Old Testament prophecies. He spoke from morning until evening, and when he was done, some were convinced, but others refused to believe.

I suspect that the unbelievers consisted mostly of people who had already made up their minds. They were much like those who had dragged Jesus before Pilate. They hated Jesus without cause.

Most people who are in leadership for any length of time eventually encounter people who hate them without cause. Most leaders experience criticism rooted in jealousy, envy, and spite. Learning how to deal with unjust criticism is one of the most important lessons a leader must learn.

How to Handle Criticism

As you read the account of the life of Jesus, you get the impression that he was never surprised or greatly troubled by criticism. He never became defensive. He never complained about the unfairness of it all. He never seemed intimidated by his opponents. Perhaps because he understood the wickedness of human hearts, he simply expected unfair criticism as a fact of life.

I have to confess that I have never become accustomed to criticism. I suspect you haven't either. The most hurtful criticism of all is that which comes from other Christians.

A friend of mine, a Christian layman, once taught a large adult Sunday school class on the book of Genesis. He was teaching from Genesis 2:15, "The Lord God took the man and put him in the garden of Eden to work it and keep it," when he made a statement that some in the class considered controversial. He said that God had given the human race a responsibility to be good stewards of the earth and that we should take good care of the environment.

Some in the class thought this man had injected politics into the Bible study, and they took offense. Unfortunately, those who were offended didn't raise their concerns openly in the class or face-to-face with the teacher. They criticized the teacher by gossiping and complaining about him behind his back.

After this man found out what was being said about him, he told me, "I expect people outside the church to criticize me. But it sure hurts when your brothers and sisters in Christ do it—and what hurts even worse is when I have to hear about the criticism secondhand."

Because Jesus was God as well as man, and therefore perfect, all the criticism he received was unjust criticism. But you and I, being fallible and fallen, receive a lot of criticism that is justified, constructive, and good for us to hear. As Orlando Magic cofounder Pat Williams observed, "Wise leaders hunger for constructive criticism more than praise because criticism instructs; praise does not." [3] He goes on to say that leaders should have an intentional strategy for welcoming criticism:

> Invite people to come to you directly with any complaints about your leadership. When people know they can come to you and voice any concern without fear of retribution, they will have no need to complain about you on the office grapevine. In fact, they will praise you behind your back for being so approachable. [4]

The apostle Paul understood the need for leaders to be open to constructive criticism. During his early ministry, before undertaking his three missionary journeys, Paul went to Jerusalem with Barnabas and Titus to meet with the church leaders there "and set before them…the gospel that I proclaim among the Gentiles, in order to make sure I was not running or had not run in vain" (Galatians 2:2b). In other words, Paul was preaching the gospel to the Gentiles, and he wanted the church leaders in Jerusalem to hear his message and critique it, to make sure he was not preaching something false.

Paul preached that faith in Jesus Christ frees us from bondage to the Law of Moses. This message was new, daring, and scandalous to legalistic Judaism, so Paul wanted the affirmation of the church leaders in Jerusalem. When he explained his message before the leaders of the church, they supported him. He had invited criticism, but the church leaders did not criticize his message. His gospel, which was given to Paul by Jesus himself, passed the test.

Sometime later, as Paul relates in Galatians 2, the apostle Peter (also known as Cephas) visited the church in Antioch, Syria. At one point, Peter separated himself from the Gentile believers in Antioch and ate his meals only with other Jewish Christians. Paul confronted Peter and told him that his conduct was hypocritical and out of step with the gospel. Peter, a wise leader who welcomed criticism, received Paul's words of constructive criticism and changed his behavior.

Though Paul welcomed constructive criticism, he let the unjust criticism of his enemies roll off his back. In another letter, Paul said to anyone who opposed his ministry, "But with me it is a very small thing that I should be judged by you or by any human court. In fact, I do not even judge myself. For I am not aware of anything against myself, but I am not thereby acquitted. It is the Lord who judges me" (1 Corinthians 4:3-4).

Paul didn't worry about pleasing other people, especially his enemies. He was focused on pleasing the Lord. Since the Lord's judgment of him was the only opinion that mattered, he was able to shrug off the criticism and judgmental opinions of others. Being criticized by his opponents was "a very small thing" to Paul because being approved by God was *everything* to him.

How to Respond to Critics and Criticism

All leaders are subject to criticism. Much of that criticism is unjust, cruel, destructive, and even anonymous. It's hard to know how to respond to unjust criticism. Should you answer it? Fight back? Offer a reasoned defense? Or simply ignore it? It takes a great deal of wisdom and spiritual maturity to know how to respond to unjust criticism as Jesus would.

When his opponents criticized him for doing good on the Sabbath, Jesus responded with calm logic and sound biblical reasoning. When they criticized him for allowing his disciples to eat with hands that had not been ceremonially washed, he bluntly called them hypocrites, quoted Scripture, and showed how the religious leaders placed man-made traditions above the commandments of God (see Mark 7:1-23). When they challenged his authority, he would often answer a question with a question: "Was the baptism of John [the Baptist] from heaven or from man?"—he knew they didn't dare answer honestly because they feared the people (see Luke 20:1-8).

But very often, Jesus simply refused to respond to criticism. When the religious leaders dragged Jesus before Pontius Pilate and accused him of "misleading our nation and forbidding us to give tribute to Caesar, and saying that he himself is Christ, a king," Jesus did not respond. He did not defend himself. He didn't answer the charges (which Pilate undoubtedly knew were false and contradictory). As the Old Testament prophecy described him:

> He was oppressed, and he was afflicted,
>   yet he opened not his mouth;
> like a lamb that is led to the slaughter,
>   and like a sheep that before its shearers is silent,
>   so he opened not his mouth.
>
> (Isaiah 53:7)

Sometimes the best reply to a false accusation or unjust criticism is silence. Don't even dignify a scurrilous accusation with an argument. Treat it as unworthy of your attention. Shrug it off. At other times, it may be best to counter a false accusation with logic and evidence so that you can expose and defuse it. Pray, ask God for wisdom, and make a leadership decision as to the best response to that false criticism.

But what about those times when the criticism we receive is justified—and constructive? What about those times when someone cares enough to criticize us for our own good? Let me suggest to you a three-step approach for receiving and sifting the criticism you receive as a leader so that you can learn and grow from the constructive criticism that comes your way.

Step 1: Listen

Those who practice the leadership style of Jesus are good listeners. They are willing to hear what others say, even if it's painful to listen to. They listen without interrupting, without becoming defensive, without becoming angry, and without counterattacking. Our critics may be telling us what we need to hear. Even when the criticism is harsh, we have an obligation as Christlike leaders to remain calm, controlled, open-minded, and open-hearted.

Owen Lovejoy was a Congregationalist minister and leading abolitionist who became a Republican congressman from Illinois and a close friend and ally of President Abraham Lincoln. On one occasion, President Lincoln asked Congressman Lovejoy to convey a note to the secretary of war, Edwin Stanton. This was after Stanton and Lincoln were on good speaking terms. The reason Lincoln was sending the note was simply to save himself a walk over to the War Department office. The contents of the note related to a routine wartime matter of repositioning Union regiments.

Lovejoy took the note to Stanton, who read it, and then looked up with annoyance. "Did Lincoln give you an order of that kind?"

"He did, sir," Lovejoy replied.

"Then he is a fool."

"Do you mean to say the president is a fool?"

"Yes, sir, if he gave you such an order as that."

Congressman Lovejoy returned to the White House and told the president what Stanton had said.

"Did Stanton say I was a fool?" Lincoln said.

"He did, sir, and repeated it."

Lincoln considered for a moment. Then, rising to his feet, he said, "If Stanton said I was a fool, then I must be one, for he is nearly always right, and generally says what he means. I will step over and see him." [5]

Abraham Lincoln was a wise, authentic leader who would rather listen and learn than defend himself. If you would learn and grow from the criticism you receive, then be a leader who listens.

Step 2: Ask Yourself, "Is It True?"

It's hard to receive criticism. It takes great maturity to drop our defenses and listen to someone criticize us without interrupting or defending ourselves. It's even harder to reflect objectively on that criticism and ask ourselves, "Is it true?"

In our fallen nature, we resist unpleasant truth. That's why the most common response to criticism is denial and even counterattack. We don't want to consider the possibility that we are wrong. For some of us, the very thought of admitting "I was wrong" is almost unbearable.

But we can know if criticism is justified only if we honestly search our hearts, ask the Holy Spirit to reveal his truth to us, and pray for the courage to act on the truth. When analyzing criticism, it's helpful to go to a few close, trusted friends for counsel. Say to them, "I have received criticism that I do such-and-such. I wasn't aware that I do that, and I'm struggling to understand if this is an area where I need to change. You know me well, and you've been watching my life. Do you think this criticism is justified?"

If, after objectively analyzing the criticism, we honestly conclude that the criticism is misplaced, then our next step is to ask God for the grace to withstand and bear up under the unfair criticism. The fact that someone has wrongly criticized us doesn't make that person our enemy. Even our friends can misunderstand us.

It can be especially painful when we feel unfairly criticized by a friend. We want to be liked and approved, especially by those we are close to. But sometimes we feel attacked by those we love and trust. All we can do is pray for wisdom, make peace if we can (see Romans 12:18), and ask God for the strength to continue loving and forgiving the person who criticizes us.

Ultimately, it helps to remember the words of the apostle Paul, "It is the Lord who judges me" (1 Corinthians 4:4b). If we are confident that we have put God first in our lives, then we won't have to waste precious time defending ourselves against our critics.

Step 3: Prepare for Future Criticism

A leader must always expect criticism. Some criticism will be fair and accurate, and some won't. A leader should never be caught off guard by criticism. Authentic, Christlike leaders are always ready to respond to their critics in a godly way. If we go through each day expecting criticism as a fact of leadership life, fortified by faith in God and determined not to be deterred or devastated by it, we will be able to meet criticism with confidence and grace.

I know of one woman in the business world who has armed herself for dealing with criticism. She keeps a printed prayer on her desk, next to her phone and computer, so that she can always pray this prayer whenever she receives an angry phone call or critical email: "Lord Jesus, you felt the hatred of sinners, and you loved them. Help me to love my critics with your unconditional love."

The Vocal Minority

It's easy to forget that our harshest critics often represent a tiny minority of the community we serve. Our critics are often so loud and insistent that their voices drown out all the encouragement and affirmation we receive from the vast majority of the people we influence.

I heard about a church that had been in existence for nearly a century and had experienced no significant growth throughout those years. Then a new pastor came and he began making changes. Those changes brought significant growth to the church, so that a second morning worship service had to be added. New Sunday school classrooms needed to be built.

Amid all the excitement and change taking place, critics and opponents arose. They didn't approach this pastor directly with their criticism. Instead, he would learn about the criticism when someone came to him and said, "People are saying…" The congregation was thriving and growing, yet the pastor became depressed as he kept hearing murmurs of complaint.

As time passed, the complaints became more frequent, more caustic, and more personally destructive. His depression and self-doubt grew. He lost sleep. He paced in his office, considering whether he ought to resign. He could not focus on the good he was doing. The criticism consumed his thoughts. He began to think the entire church was against him.

One day, he went to his knees in anguish and prayed for clarity and understanding. He asked God to reveal the truth to him so he would know what to do. He later explained what happened next: "Almost immediately, I realized that the complaints that filled my mind had come from just four families—the power structure that had ruled the congregation long before I became pastor. In a moment, I understood that they didn't want any change of any kind for any reason. I also realized that those four families represented a tiny minority of the congregation."

From that moment forward, the pastor was able to shrug off the complaints and criticism that came his way and to focus on the exciting ministry taking place in the church. He was finally able to hear the encouraging words from the majority of church members. When he asked God to reveal the truth, he finally realized he had nothing to fear from a vocal minority.

While it's important to listen to the voices of our critics so that we can learn and grow from valid criticism, we also need a godly sense of perspective. We need to distinguish between a vocal minority and the often-silent majority—and we need to remember that it's the majority that counts.

Jesus had that perspective. He had no illusions about his critics and persecutors, but he did not let the vocal minority divert him from his mission. As Mark's gospel tells us, "And the great throng heard him gladly" (Mark 12:37). The opponents of Jesus were a vocal minority who opposed change. Jesus threatened their corrupt power, and his popularity made them envious and murderous.

When we as leaders encounter criticism, it's important for us to ask ourselves a few questions so that we avoid being thrown into emotional turmoil by a strident but tiny minority:

- Where does this criticism come from?
- Is everyone against me? Or merely a few malcontents?
- Is there truth in this criticism—even a little?
- What (if anything) do I need to learn from this criticism?

One of the key roles of a leader is to be a catalyst for change. In every organization, team, or church, there are those who resist change. So if a leader tries to introduce something new—a new vision, a new set of goals, new rules, or a new methodology—there will inevitably be resistance from the old guard. Critics will complain—sometimes to your face, but more often behind your back.

As a leader of all the people in your organization, you have an obligation to care for your critics as well as your supporters. Try to include them in your optimistic vision for the future. Do what you can to allay their fears and reservations. If possible, find ways to get them to buy in to your new ideas, new agenda, and new plans for the future. You may be able to mute some of the criticism.

But ultimately, a leader must lead. As we follow the leadership style of Jesus, we see that a leader must keep moving forward, even against a barrage of criticism and opposition. Jesus faced intense, murderous hostility in his leadership life, but he didn't let anything stand between him and the victorious accomplishment of his mission.

Once when I was experiencing some opposition in my leadership role, a friend told me, "Maybe you ought to feel good when people criticize you." Feel *good*? That didn't make sense to me. I asked him why I should feel good about being criticized.

"Remember what Jesus said," he replied. "'Blessed are you when others revile you and persecute you and utter all kinds of evil against you falsely on my account. Rejoice and be glad, for your reward is great in heaven, for so they persecuted the prophets who were before you'" (Matthew 5:11-12). That was some of the best leadership advice I've ever received.

Just before Jesus went to the cross, he told his disciples, "Remember the word that I said to you: 'A servant is not greater than his master.' If they persecuted me, they will also persecute you. If they kept my word, they will also keep yours" (John 15:20). This is wise leadership counsel from the lips of the Master himself.

As you follow the leadership style of Jesus, expect criticism and opposition, just as he did. When you are criticized, listen to it. If it is valid, learn from it. And if it is unjust, remember this leadership principle:

Principle 15

Only one leader was ever perfect,
and they criticized him too.

16   Molehills and Mountains

A few years ago, Tom (not his real name) took an executive position with a well-known organization. He had a successful track record at his previous job and was looking forward to his new position. A committed Christian, Tom was a dedicated practitioner of the leadership style of Jesus.

After six months with that organization, Tom resigned in disgust. He couldn't take it anymore.

Someone asked Tom why he quit after only six months on the job. "Pettiness," Tom replied. "That entire organization was infested with office politics, jealousy, and rivalries. Everybody in the organization was trying to one-up everyone else. I wanted to be part of the team, but there was no team! I was expected to align myself with one of the factions in the organization. Any word of support for one person made me an instant enemy to someone else. I tried to preach teamwork and cooperation, but pettiness was too deeply ingrained in the culture of that organization."

Many companies, organizations, teams, and churches are so focused on the big issues that they fail to notice they are being undermined by petty issues—by personality clashes, turf wars, jealousy, whisper campaigns, and the like. Seemingly minor problems can be hugely destructive to an organization's morale and effectiveness.

It's a leader's job to look at the big picture, to see the mountain, and to lead the organization to the summit. Unfortunately, all too many leaders never reach the mountaintop because they get tripped up by molehills.

Petty People

Petty leaders tend to produce petty organizations that become divided and conflicted over petty issues. There are several kinds of "molehill leaders"—leaders who major on the minor and stumble over molehills. These include:

The Promises-Promises Leader

Many leaders continually stir up conflict by making promises they cannot or will not keep. "If there's anything you want, just ask," they say. Ten minutes later, that promise is forgotten. This kind of leader likes to be liked and makes contradictory promises to opposing factions in order to be liked by both sides. Result: he ends up in the middle of a turf war with *both* sides mad at him.

The Bureaucratic Leader

Many people in leadership positions are not true leaders by temperament. They are bureaucrats who exercise authority in strict accordance to a set of rules. It doesn't matter to a bureaucrat if his performance actually makes his organization more effective, more profitable, or more successful. All that matters is that he faithfully and unerringly adheres to the rules. If someone suggests a new and more effective way of doing things, a bureaucrat will say, "We can't do it that way. We've never done it that way before. The rules don't allow that." Leaders are visionary people who promote change and improvement. Bureaucrats maintain the status quo.

The First-Thing-Tomorrow Leader

The classic procrastinator is always busy yet never seems to get anything done on time. He manages to spend so much time on petty issues that he is never able to prioritize his most important goals. As a result, he is constantly overpromising and under-delivering.

Whenever you ask him about the status of an important project, his answer is, "I'll get right on that—first thing tomorrow."

The Glad-I-Thought-of-That Leader

These petty leaders insist that their fingerprints be on everything and that no one else shares credit. If someone else has a suggestion or idea, this type of leader rejects it. It's not a good idea unless he initiates it. If there is a way for him to get credit for your idea, then he will happily do so and say, "Glad I thought of that!" This type of leader reasons, "What good is an idea if I can't claim credit?"

The What's-in-It-for-Me Leader

Petty leaders usually look out for Number One. They are not primarily interested in the success of the organization or their followers. They want to know, "What's in it for me?" They won't support any idea, suggestion, program, plan, or goal that doesn't benefit them personally. Many petty leaders are master manipulators and are quite adept at maneuvering a group discussion toward a conclusion that benefits them.

There are many other types of petty leaders—the cynic, the gossip, the self-appointed expert, the bully, and more. Organizations tend to reflect the character of their leaders. So it's no surprise that petty leaders are usually found heading up organizations that are torn by petty strife, conflict, confusion over priorities, lack of vision, and low morale.

Any organization can become preoccupied with pettiness—a business, a nonprofit organization, a church, a school, a political group, a committee, an athletic team, or even a military unit. Authentic leaders help their followers catch the big vision, pursue important priorities and goals, and support one another. Where authentic Christlike leadership thrives, pettiness dies.

How Jesus Dealt with Pettiness

When Jesus caught his disciples bickering about who was the

greatest, he confronted their pettiness head-on. That's what great leaders do. They inspire greatness, and they focus their followers' attention on the things that truly matter. When followers are focused on climbing the mountain, they have no time for molehills.

The apostle John recorded another time when Jesus rebuked the petty behavior of one of his followers. It occurred during the Lord's third postresurrection appearance to the disciples beside the Sea of Galilee (Lake Tiberias). Jesus restored Simon Peter after his cowardly defection before the crucifixion. Then Jesus prophesied to Peter that he would glorify God by dying a martyr's death.

As you can imagine, Peter was not exactly overjoyed to hear about his future martyrdom. Seeing that his fellow apostle John was following close behind them and eavesdropping on their conversation, Peter said to Jesus, "Lord, what about this man?"

It was a petty question. Simon Peter was saying to Jesus, "If I have to die a martyr's death, shouldn't he have to die a martyr's death too? I mean, Lord, it just wouldn't be fair if I had to go through the agony of being, say, crucified upside down while John gets to pass away quietly in his sleep."

Jesus replied, "If it is my will that he remain until I come, what is that to you? You follow me!" (see John 20:20-23). In other words, "Stop being petty. John answers to me, Peter, not to you. So mind your own business. Focus on following me."

As leaders, we need to remember that we cannot and should not treat everyone in the organization alike. Yes, we should try to treat everyone fairly, but that's not the same thing as treating everybody alike. Some people in your organization work harder or have greater experience and skills and should have greater rewards. When people with a petty attitude complain and say, "That's not fair," the leader has no obligation to explain or defend his decisions. It is enough to say, "Mind your own business and stop being petty. Focus on doing your own job well."

The leaders of the early church learned from the leadership

example of Jesus. When pettiness and conflict threatened the unity of the early church, church leaders met the problems head-on and solved them. We see this principle early in the book of Acts. As the early church grew, a conflict arose between Christians from two cultures, the Jewish culture and the Hellenist or Greek culture. The church had a compassionate ministry of providing food and assistance to widows, and the Greek Christians thought the Jewish Christian hierarchy was neglecting the Greek widows.

So the apostles, the leaders in the church, called a meeting and told the people of the church, "It is not right that we should give up preaching the word of God to serve tables. Therefore, brothers, pick out from among you seven men of good repute, full of the Spirit and of wisdom, whom we will appoint to this duty. But we will devote ourselves to prayer and to the ministry of the word" (Acts 6:2b-4).

In other words, "We need to get our priorities straight. As apostles, as leaders, we need to focus on Jesus's number one priority, which is preaching and evangelism. But we also need to make sure that our widows are cared for, so let's pick seven wise, Spirit-filled men to carry out this duty." The apostles made sure that the church remained focused on its vision, the Great Commission, while also making sure that human needs were met. It was a wise decision, and it reflected the leadership style of Jesus.

The apostle Paul also practiced the leadership style of Jesus and continually battled pettiness among believers. In his letter to the church at Philippi, he wrote:

> I entreat Euodia and I entreat Syntyche to agree in the Lord. Yes, I ask you also, true companion, help these women, who have labored side by side with me in the gospel together with Clement and the rest of my fellow workers, whose names are in the book of life (Philippians 4:2-3).

We don't know the reason for the disagreement between these

two women in the Philippian church. It might have been a clash over differing views of ministry, or it might have been a simple clash of personalities. Sometimes two people are just so different—or so much alike—that they simply can't get along. But people who are in the same church, in the same organization, or on the same team have to learn to get along whether they like it or not.

When Paul writes, "I entreat Euodia and I entreat Syntyche to agree in the Lord," he is not necessarily saying they have to reach an identical opinion. That is not always possible. But two people who serve the same Lord can always agree in the Lord to put their relationship in Christ ahead of their differences. They can disagree over methods, programs, issues, and even secondary points of doctrine—and they can even *dislike* each other!—while agreeing in the Lord to love and accept one another.

Baseball player Dusty Baker had a long major-league career as an outfielder, and then as a manager. He says that his service in the Marine Corps was great preparation for his baseball career, both as a player and a manager. In the Marines, he said, "I learned a lot about teamwork." In a team environment, teammates have to be committed to each other, looking out for each other and even being willing to sacrifice themselves for each other—"even if you don't like him and he doesn't like you. That's teamwork." [1]

That's the difference between *liking* someone and *loving* someone. You can love a person you don't even like. You can even love people you can't stand. How is that possible? The answer is found in the Greek word *agape* (pronounced *ah-GAH-pay*). Most people think of love as a feeling or an emotion, but Christlike *agape*-love is a decision we make. When we choose to accept someone we don't even like, we are practicing *agape*-love. We are agreeing together with that person in the Lord.

Whether we *like* someone or not is a petty matter. But whether we truly *love* one another is the heart and soul of the Christian faith.

If we persevere in Christlike love, we will always stay focused on what truly matters.

The conflict between Euodia and Syntyche, and Paul's excellent advice to them, brings us to our next leadership principle:

Principle 16

Wise leaders keep petty problems
from growing into major problems.

Part 5

The **Future** of Leadership

17   Where Leaders Come From

Why did Jesus choose the Twelve?

What criteria did he use in selecting those twelve original disciples? Did he actually see leadership potential in them that he thought was worth developing? Or did he pick a dozen unexceptional men, and then impart special abilities to them to prove what he could create out of common human clay?

After the day of Pentecost, when the Holy Spirit came upon them, those disciples became amazingly bold, brave, and eloquent. They demonstrated gifts and abilities they had never shown before. But how much potential did they actually have at the beginning, when Jesus first said to them, "Follow me"?

I honestly don't know. But my guess is that Jesus didn't pick the disciples at random. I suspect that he saw some rough, unrefined leadership qualities in them before he called them.

Take Andrew, for example. John's gospel tells us that Andrew was a disciple of John the Baptist before he met Jesus (see John 1:35-40). Clearly, Andrew was a man who hungered for spiritual truth, which is a sign of great potential. And Andrew's brother Simon Peter also stands out as a man of great enthusiasm, a natural spokesman for the group, and a man with keen spiritual insight and bold faith (he was only the second man in history to walk on water). Even though Peter was also prone to acting rashly and speaking before thinking, he demonstrated the boldness and decisiveness of a leader.

It's easy to imagine that Jesus saw positive qualities in Andrew and Peter and readily recognized their leadership potential. And I suspect that Jesus saw similar leadership traits in the rest of the Twelve. Ultimately, as he mentored and taught them and then sent them out to do ministry, he refined those traits and transformed their weaknesses into strengths.

We can learn a lot from Jesus and the way he recruited and trained his disciples. As a leader yourself, you have probably faced the challenge of trying to recruit people to your team, church, or organization who can step up and lead—and you have probably faced disappointment and discouragement.

Perhaps you have been looking for leaders in the wrong places. Or perhaps you have been applying the wrong criteria in your search.

Looking for Leaders in the Wrong Places

Where do we usually look for leaders? We look for them in leadership positions. We don't want to take a chance on somebody who has never led before. So we follow the saying, "If you want something done, ask a busy person." We keep going to the same people again and again, asking them to lead. Pastors keep calling on the same lay leaders to head committees. CEOs keep calling on the same managers to take charge of projects. Coaches keep calling on the same players to provide leadership to the offense or the defense.

This approach works for a while, but eventually these few leaders become overworked. They experience burnout. If they leave, there's no one to step up and take their place. When that happens, the failure is not theirs, it's ours. We as leaders have failed to identify, recruit, mentor, and develop new leaders. The raw material is there, but we have failed to call it forth.

There is latent leadership potential all around us, but we don't see it. Instead, we wait for the emergence of proven leadership.

One leadership organization conducted an informal poll at one of their conferences to find out how the attendees had become leaders. The results: 5 percent had leadership thrust upon them in a moment of crisis; 10 percent had risen to leadership because they felt naturally gifted as leaders; but the overwhelming majority, 85 percent, had become leaders due to the influence of another leader. They emerged as leaders because another established leader had modeled leadership to them and had mentored them in the principles of leadership.[1]

If you look at Jesus and the disciples he chose, you would see a similar statistic. Of the Twelve, only one—Peter—seems to be naturally gifted as a leader. He is the only one who has the kind of forceful, assertive personality one associates with natural leadership ability. Subtract Judas Iscariot, the traitor in the group, and you are left with ten disciples out of twelve, or 83 percent of the entire group. The 83 percent became leaders due to the influence of Jesus, an established leader who modeled leadership and mentored them.

So if you want to find leaders, you should do so according to the leadership style of Jesus. Instead of identifying a few strong natural leaders and working them to the point of burnout, I suggest you do what Jesus did: Look at your followers from a whole new perspective. Look at the quieter people, the people who don't stand out as much from the crowd, but who have skills and interests and talents that could be powerful assets in a leadership role.

Consider Matthew (Levi) the tax collector. Why did Jesus choose him to be one of the Twelve? He didn't have a charming or charismatic personality. He was bitterly resented by his fellow Jews because he collaborated with the hated Roman oppressors. Before his conversion to Christ, Matthew was a man of ambition and initiative who willingly endured the scorn of his countrymen in order to make money. But as a follower of Christ, his focus changed—and many of his personality flaws were transformed into strengths. He was still a hard worker—but now he was ambitious for the gospel instead of personal gain. He was still hardened to scorn—but now he would endure scorn for the sake of the gospel instead of the Roman government. Jesus recognized Matthew's unique traits, including his flaws, as leadership potential.

We know that Jesus recognized the tempestuous enthusiasm of James and John because he nicknamed them "the sons of thunder." Jesus also recognized the radical commitment and fervor of Simon the Zealot as leadership potential. He recognized a kind of no-nonsense, roughhewn leadership strength in Andrew and the other fishermen. After recruiting these men, he mentored them individually and as a group. He built their confidence and their faith. He showed them how to practice and sharpen their leadership skills. He taught them in parables and asked them open-ended questions to provoke and refine their thinking.

As you recruit leaders in your organization or team, you may be looking for Peters and missing out on the less obvious leaders in your organization, the people like Matthew, James, John, Andrew, Simon, and the rest. As you look at the people in your organization, look harder, look closer, and see if you don't discover a diamond in the rough, a person with latent potential just waiting to hear you say, "I think you can lead."

We know very little about the background, qualifications, and personality of most of the disciples. But we do know this: Every one of those men (with the exception of Judas Iscariot) was trained by Jesus and became a leader. (And even Judas was there to serve a divine purpose.)

Discovering Leadership Where You Least Expect It

Jesus didn't wait for leadership to announce itself. He didn't administer personality inventories or ask his disciples to write up their résumés. With his infallible insight, he looked closely at each person, looking for signs of hidden leadership potential. When he saw the potential in someone, he said, "Come, follow me."

You and I don't have infallible insight. A few of the people we select and call as potential leaders will undoubtedly disappoint us and wash out as leaders. But if we are willing to look closely at every individual, as Jesus did, we will assemble a stronger, more talented team. When we seek out only the obvious born leaders, we assemble a leadership team of strong-minded, strong-willed, forceful personalities who are all pretty much alike in most respects. But if we will seek out the less obvious leaders-in-the-rough, we will assemble a diverse mix of abilities, gifts, and strengths—and we will have a much stronger leadership team as a result.

Leaders often complain that there are not enough people in their company, church, team, or organization to meet its leadership needs. I disagree. I think there are plenty of potential leaders in every group. We just haven't identified them yet. That's the challenge we face as leaders, and the answer to that challenge is found in the leadership style of Jesus, in the way he identified and developed leadership traits among his followers.

I know of one medium-sized suburban church where the pastor became accustomed to relying on one particular couple for leadership in a variety of church ministries and programs. One day, the couple told the pastor they would be moving out of state. The woman had been diagnosed with a health problem that required her to live in a warmer climate. The pastor was in shock. These two people were the backbone of the lay leadership in the church. He considered them irreplaceable. There was no one else in the church to step up and lead as they had. Or so he thought.

The pastor went before the congregation and made an appeal from the pulpit. He talked about all the years of service this couple had given to the church, and now they were leaving. "As a result," he said, "we need people who are willing to volunteer to take over their responsibilities."

To the pastor's amazement, eight people responded, moved into the leadership roles vacated by this couple, and they all performed brilliantly. They brought with them an array of new talents, new gifts, and new ideas that reinvigorated the church's ministry. The pastor learned several important lessons from this experience:

First, no one is indispensable. When one or two leaders step down, God can raise up many more.

Second, many people are unaware of their leadership abilities. They don't see themselves as leaders. They are just waiting for an established leader to discover them, affirm them, and give them an opportunity to lead.

Third, in every organization there are hidden leaders who will emerge and excel in leadership when they know they are wanted and needed.

Fourth, most leaders learn on the job. If you want to develop leaders in your organization, give them work to do.

On-the-Job Leadership Training

Jesus understood his mission. He knew his time with the disciples was limited. He would have to train them, mentor them, and transform them into leaders before he left this earth. Near the end of the gospel of John, Jesus clearly knows they are ready, so he commissions them: "As the Father has sent me, even so I am sending you" (John 20:21b).

The disciples' first big test came soon after Jesus left them. Great crowds had gathered in Jerusalem for Pentecost, the Jewish Feast of Weeks. Peter stood before the crowd and preached one of the greatest sermons in history. As a result, three thousand people received Jesus as Lord and Savior, and they were baptized and added to the church.

When the religious leaders heard about this, they threatened the disciples and commanded them not to preach anymore. But the disciples knew they had to obey God, not man, so they continued preaching. Finally, Peter and John were arrested and brought before the religious council—the very same group of corrupt leaders who had plotted the death of Jesus. Just a few weeks earlier, Peter had denied his Lord and gone into hiding out of fear of these men. Now he stood boldly before them, completely unafraid, preaching Christ to the very men who had murdered Christ (see Acts 4:1-12).

Hearing Peter preach, the religious leaders were amazed. As the book of Acts records, "Now when they saw the boldness of Peter and John, and perceived that they were uneducated, common men, they were astonished. And they recognized that they had been with Jesus" (Acts 4:13). The religious leaders were astonished because they thought they knew what leadership looked like. They thought the only true leaders were highly educated, ambitious, power-obsessed men like themselves. Yet here were these unlearned working-class fishermen, and they were preaching with authority and boldness! And the religious leaders knew why Peter and John had undergone a leadership transformation: "they had been with Jesus."

The religious leaders tried to intimidate Peter and John, threatening them and ordering them to stop preaching about Jesus. But the two apostles replied, "Whether it is right in the sight of God to listen to you rather than to God, you must judge, for we cannot but speak of what we have seen and heard" (Acts 4:19b-20).

The transformation of the disciples into bold and authoritative leaders is all the more amazing because Jesus didn't choose a dozen natural-born leaders. Instead, he chose a dozen ordinary blue-collar working stiffs, put them through an intense mentoring and leadership training program, and radically transformed them into a force that would impact the world.

The religious leaders looked at these men and saw nothing special in them—no talent, no ability, no education, no aptitude for leadership. Jesus looked at them and saw limitless potential. He called them, saying, "Follow me," and then he refined their potential through on-the-job training.

How to Choose a Leader

What should you look for when recruiting new leaders? I suggest you look for qualities that are difficult to teach. You can teach a person such skills as decision-making, strategic planning, team-building, public speaking, conflict resolution, conducting meetings, and so forth. If a raw recruit lacks these skills, that's no problem. These are all learnable skills.

But some other traits are difficult, if not impossible, to teach. It's hard to teach someone to be a person of character and integrity if they lack those traits. It's hard to teach someone to exhibit a strong work ethic if they did not learn the value of hard work early in life. It's hard to take someone who is self-centered and immoral and to transform that person into a role model. And it's hard to take someone who is disloyal and undependable and turn that person into a faithful leader.

So when recruiting new leaders, look for character qualities, integrity, hard work, moral virtue, and faithfulness. You can easily build leadership skills and competencies on a foundation of strong character.

In the Lord's Parable of the Talents, Jesus tells us of a master who praises his profitable servant, saying, "Well done, good and faithful servant. You have been faithful over a little; I will set you over much" (see Matthew 25:23). It is faithfulness, not leadership skill, that Jesus praises in this story.

You may think it's hard to recruit people with good skills. But I guarantee it is even harder to recruit people with good character. It's even harder to recruit people who will work faithfully behind the scenes, doing all the little thankless tasks that need to be done, people with the heart of a servant and the wisdom of a leader.

As you search for leaders within your organization, church, or team, be sure to pray for wisdom. Before you start talking to potential candidates, talk to God and ask him for the supernatural insight to make a wise choice.

I once heard of a church that offered twenty-one Sunday school classes for adults and children. In the spring, more than half the teachers informed the Sunday school superintendent that they would not be back to teach in the fall. The superintendent faced a mass exodus of teachers and had no idea where to recruit new ones.

The superintendent's first impulse was to panic. But he talked to his pastor, and the pastor suggested prayer. "Pray for wisdom," the pastor said, "and I'll pray with you." So they prayed together, and the sense of panic passed. Within a few weeks, new leaders emerged and soon every class had a teacher. As the apostle James reminds us, "If any of you lacks wisdom, let him ask God, who gives generously to all without reproach, and it will be given him" (James 1:5).

Always remember that at least 85 percent of your potential leaders are as yet unrecognized, have never been called, and are just waiting for you to tell them, "I think you can lead." They have spiritual gifts that are not being used (for more on spiritual gifts, see Romans 12:3-8, 1 Corinthians 12 and 14, and Ephesians 4:7-16).

As you mentor and train leaders, be sure to affirm them. That doesn't mean you should hand out empty praise and flattery. Instead, when you see them exercising Christlike character and Christlike leadership traits, tell them you see them taking on the character and traits of a leader. Mention specific examples of things they have said and done as evidence of their leadership growth. Focus on evidence of faith and character instead of accomplishments.

Jesus affirmed his disciples by calling them friends, by commending them on their righteous works and their faith, and by trusting them with increasingly more responsibility (see John 13:10; 15:14-15; 20:21; 21:15-17). When Jesus affirmed his followers, he increased their confidence. He empowered them to believe they could take on the world.

And in the book of Acts, they did take on the world—and they influenced and changed the world for Christ. In all the annals of leadership history, there has never been a more effective way of recruiting, training, and commissioning leaders than the process Jesus demonstrated in the gospels. As leaders, our task is not merely to collect a group of followers but to raise up a new generation of leaders. That brings us to our next leadership principle:

Principle 17

Leaders are chosen and gifted by God,
but we have to discover and develop them.

18   Turning Followers into Leaders

once studied John chapters 13 through 17 because I wanted to meditate on the last words Jesus spoke to his disciples before his arrest. As I read, I was struck by the fact that this was so much more than the Lord's farewell to his followers. It was actually a summary and a reminder of their three-year leadership apprenticeship with him.

During the weeks leading up to his arrest, trial, and crucifixion, Jesus had been telling them gently that they would soon be on their own. He told them he wanted them to love one another and serve one another. He urged them to abide in him and obey his commandments. He warned them that the world would hate them and persecute them. He told them their sorrow would turn to joy, and he would send them a Helper, the Holy Spirit. And he prayed that the Father would guard them, unify them, and sanctify them, and that the world would believe in him because of their message.

It was hard for the disciples to understand these final words of Jesus. When he told them he was going to die, they seemed to be in denial. Much of what he said was baffling to them at the time, and they understood it only later, after the resurrection.

I believe it was hard for Jesus to say these things to these men he had mentored, discipled, and loved for three years. Soon they would have to go on without his physical presence to guide them. He knew how painful the next few days would be for them.

We tend to think of Jesus in his role as Savior and Lord, the One who came to die on the cross in our place to save us from our sins. But that was only part of the Lord's mission. He also came to establish his church, and he did that by raising up twelve leaders, twelve disciples, twelve apostles. He selected them, called them, taught them, commissioned them, and put them into ministry. He tossed them into situations where they had to sink or swim—and sometimes they sank.

Ultimately, they all (with the exception of Judas Iscariot) learned their leadership lessons well, and they went on to spend the rest of their lives in service to the Lord. They became the first official members of a church that would eventually encompass the globe. And they became the first practitioners of the leadership style of Jesus.

One of the key lessons we learn from the leadership life of Jesus is that the purpose of leadership is not to produce followers, but to produce more leaders. If a leader is not continually recruiting, inspiring, training, and sending out new leaders, then that leader is not truly leading. A leader who produces only followers is just a boss.

A leader who is constantly trying to turn followers into leaders helps to guarantee the vitality and longevity of his organization. With this leadership model, Jesus founded an organization—the church—that has grown, spread, and lived on over a span of two thousand years, with no end in sight. During the three years that Jesus trained, taught, and led the Twelve, do you think any of them foresaw what would become of their little movement? Hardly.

Yet Jesus told them they were on the ground floor of something far beyond their imagination. He said, "Truly, truly, I say to you, whoever believes in me will also do the works that I do; and greater works than these will he do, because I am going to the Father" (John 14:12). God's power, working through Jesus, healed the sick and gave sight to the blind. That same power, working through generations of Christians, changed the course of history.

One of your most important goals as a leader should be to prepare your followers to outdo you. Prepare them to do greater works than you have done. Prepare them to ascend to greater heights than you have climbed. Prepare them to achieve and succeed far beyond what they can now imagine.

Prepare them to be leaders.

They're Ready Before They Know It

As you read through the gospel account, you see Jesus commissioning his disciples to go out and do the work that he has been doing, from preaching the gospel to healing the sick. When he commissioned them, I'm sure some of them must have protested, "But I'm not ready to preach! I've never done that before. And I certainly don't know anything about healing the sick!"

But Jesus sent them out anyway. He had taught them well. He had been a role model for them. They had watched him closely. It was only natural that they would lack confidence, but Jesus knew they could do it. So he sent them out into the world, and they came back amazed at what God had done through them.

I believe that, as leaders, we need to give our followers responsibility *before* they feel ready for it. We need to put them into leadership while their confidence is still a bit shaky, while their knees are still knocking and their voices still quavering. I'm not suggesting we should push untrained people into positions they're not qualified for. But people are usually able to lead long before they *feel* ready to lead. They will protest, "But I'm not ready to lead. After I attend another seminar or read another book, I may be ready. But for now, you'd better find someone else."

What your reluctant followers are expressing is not a lack of ability but a lack of confidence. And the best way for people to gain confidence is to tackle the challenge that scares them. As Ralph Waldo Emerson said, "Do the thing you fear, and the death of fear is certain." When people tackle an intimidating challenge *and they succeed*, their confidence grows. And if they fail, they'll learn lessons from their failure.

The only way an inexperienced leader can gain experience is by doing. So encourage them to take on leadership challenges, ready or not. Tell them, "I know you don't think you're ready, but I know you are. I have enough confidence in you for both of us. Sure, you have a lot to learn. Everybody does. Start leading now, and then learn as you lead. You're going to be amazed at what an effective leader you already are."

The "sink or swim" approach really works. I know a man who, along with his wife, adopted four brothers from overseas. They ranged in age from four to nine, and they had never had an opportunity to stretch themselves and take on new challenges. Whenever this man asked his sons to try something new, they said, "We can't do that!"

To build the boys' confidence, the man signed his sons up for swimming lessons at the community pool. All four boys were horrified when they found out. "But we can't swim!" they protested.

On the day of the first lesson, the swimming teacher literally had to toss the boys into the water—they wouldn't go into the pool any other way. They landed in the water and immediately sank. The teacher patiently taught them how to float, tread water, and swim. Along the way, those four boys swallowed a lot of water.

The littlest boy, the four-year-old, caught on first. As the dad explained it, "The little guy grew gills and started paddling all around the pool. He shamed the older boys into being more adventuresome. Finally, they all got it."

Within a few years, those boys who had said, "We can't swim," became competitive swimmers, competing in swim meets around the state.

If you wait until people feel they're ready for a challenge, you'll have a long wait. But if you encourage them to take on leadership challenges *before* they think they're ready, they'll learn on the job, acquire new skills and confidence—and they will achieve great things.

I recently heard a story about Speedy Morris, the longtime head basketball coach at La Salle University in Philadelphia. Now retired, Morris recalls that his coaching career began while he was in high school, playing on the varsity basketball team. The elementary school basketball team had no coach, so the school administrator asked Speedy if he would fill in as coach. Speedy was reluctant because it meant quitting the varsity team, and he loved to play basketball.

Speedy asked his coach for advice, and his coach told him, "I know how much you love to play the game, but if you'd be willing to set aside your desire to play, you'd be doing a wonderful thing in the lives of those young boys. It would be a real act of service." Speedy Morris decided to coach the elementary school team. He continued coaching, first as an amateur, then as a professional, and he remained in coaching until his retirement, more than fifty years later.

"I never regretted the decision," he later said. "Next to a young athlete's own parents, few people can have a greater long-term impact on a young athlete's life than a coach."[1]

So identify leaders early, train them well, and give them responsibility before they think they're ready. You'll be doing your organization, and your young leaders, a big favor.

The Biblical Pattern of Leadership Development

As we study the Old Testament, we see that God employed this same approach when he raised up leaders in Israel. He chose people who felt inadequate and unprepared, and he thrust them into the great crises of history. The people God chose as leaders invariably achieved far more than they ever thought possible.

In the book of Exodus, God called Moses to lead his people out of slavery in Egypt. In his first conversation with God, Moses was full of excuses for why he was not ready to lead. He said the people wouldn't listen to him and wouldn't believe him. In reply, God gave Moses the power to do miracles that would convince the people.

Then Moses protested, "Oh, my Lord, I am not eloquent...I am slow of speech and of tongue." God replied that he, the sovereign Lord who had invented man's mouth, would give Moses the words to say.

Finally, Moses ran out of excuses and simply begged God, "Oh, my Lord, please send someone else." But God overcame all the objections and excuses of Moses, sent him into the presence of Pharaoh, and turned a reluctant man into one of the greatest leaders of all time (see Exodus 3:1–4:17).

We see a similar situation when God chose Jeremiah to be his prophet and a leader in Israel. God spoke to Jeremiah and told him, "Before I formed you in the womb I knew you, and before you were born I consecrated you; I appointed you a prophet to the nations."

Like Moses, Jeremiah was reluctant and replied, "Ah, Lord GOD! Behold, I do not know how to speak, for I am only a youth."

But the Lord was ready for Jeremiah's excuses. He said, "Do not say, 'I am only a youth'; for to all to whom I send you, you shall go, and whatever I command you, you shall speak" (see Jeremiah 1:4-7).

Most of the great leaders of ancient Israel practiced a Christlike leadership style, mentoring and instructing new leaders who would one day step into their sandals and carry on their ministry.

As Moses led the nation of Israel, he had Joshua at his side. Joshua not only assisted Moses and carried out military strategy under Moses, but he also learned principles of leadership from Moses. After the death of Moses, Joshua commanded the nation of Israel. And as the book of Joshua shows, he led faithfully and righteously.

The prophet Elijah had a powerful leadership ministry in the Northern Kingdom, and his constant companion was his protégé, Elisha. At the end of Elijah's life, as recorded in 2 Kings 2, Elijah and Elisha made a miraculous crossing of the River Jordan (the water divided and they crossed on dry land). Then a chariot of fire appeared, and Elijah was taken up in a whirlwind. As he was taken away, his mantle (the cape-like vestment of his office as prophet) fell from his shoulders onto the ground. Elisha picked up Elijah's mantle, symbolizing the transfer of the office of prophet from Elijah to Elisha.

In the New Testament, Paul followed the leadership style of Jesus by continually training and mentoring disciples who would one day replace him. These disciples included John Mark (the nephew of Barnabas), Timothy, and Priscilla and Aquila. This next generation of leaders went on to disciple more leaders. Priscilla and Aquila, for example, discipled Apollos (see Acts 18:24-28).

As Paul wrote to his spiritual son Timothy, "And what you have heard from me in the presence of many witnesses entrust to faithful men who will be able to teach others also" (2 Timothy 2:2). That is how the church grew with astonishing speed throughout the first century and how the gospel eventually spread throughout the world. And that is the key to building a growing, enduring, and forward-thinking organization, church, or team.

What Jesus Taught

In my study of the leadership style of Jesus, I have identified four methods he used to train his followers to become leaders. These methods can be used to develop leaders for any team or organization, in any field.

First, *teach precepts*. This is what most of us think of as teaching or training: instructing followers in leadership principles, imparting wisdom and knowledge, and setting forth rules of moral conduct. In the Old Testament, the prophet and judge Eli taught precepts to the boy Samuel as he served in the temple. Samuel matured and grew wise under the leadership of Eli. Eventually, Samuel succeeded Eli and became the spiritual leader of the Jewish nation.

Second, *teach by example*. In other words, be a role model so that your followers can pattern their lives after yours. Leadership is as much caught as it is taught. Followers learn their most important leadership lessons by observing their own leaders.

Ralph Waldo Emerson once wrote, "What you do speaks so

loud that I cannot hear what you say." If you convey one message through your words and an opposite message with the way you live your life, your followers will listen to your life, not your words. What you do will cancel out what you say. But if your words are in harmony with the way you live, then what you do will amplify and reinforce what you say.

Jesus lived a consistent life. He taught the truth and he modeled the truth. He was the ultimate role model. Our goal as leaders should be to pattern our example after his and give our followers a role model to look up to.

Third, *demonstrate by results*. Jesus produced results. He didn't ask people to merely take his word for it. He pointed to the results he had produced. When his opponents picked up stones to kill him, he said, "If I am not doing the works of my Father, then do not believe me; but if I do them, even though you do not believe me, believe the works, that you may know and understand that the Father is in me and I am in the Father" (John 10:37-38).

On another occasion, Jesus said, "For the works that the Father has given me to accomplish, the very works that I am doing, bear witness about me that the Father has sent me" (John 5:36). If the works that Jesus did had fallen flat, if his attempted healings had failed, if the loaves and fishes had fed only a few lucky people in the front row, Jesus could not have made the claims he did. But his claims were demonstrated by his results.

Fourth, *point to the witness of others*. Leaders need to be confirmed in their leadership role. If people do not acknowledge you as a leader, you will have no followers—and a leader without followers is not a leader.

John the Baptist bore witness of Jesus and his ministry. He announced Jesus to Israel as the Anointed One who was promised in the Old Testament. He presented Jesus to the nation as a leader.

We see this same principle in the writings of the apostle Paul, who set forth the qualifications of a leader (a bishop or overseer) in the church. Writing to Timothy, he said, "Moreover, he must be well thought of by outsiders, so that he may not fall into disgrace, into a snare of the devil" (1 Timothy 3:7). In other words, a leader in the church must be a person with a good reputation—a reputation that is affirmed even by people in the secular community.

You may think, *Why do I need the testimony of non-Christians to establish my worthiness and credibility as a leader?* It's important to remember that those who are outside the faith watch us most closely. They are looking to see if we are genuine or not. They are attentive to any little hint of hypocrisy or phoniness in our lives. So we need to live in such a way that even outsiders will be able to endorse us and give us the Good Housekeeping Seal of Approval.

A friend of mine, a pastor, discovered the importance of having a good reputation among outsiders when a newspaper editor came to interview him. The editor said, "I asked people in the community, 'Who is the most influential preacher in this county?' Your name came up again and again. I asked people another question: 'If you had only one person to trust outside your closest friends and relatives, who would you call?' Again, your name came up repeatedly."

When I heard that story, I knew that it fit. With just two questions, asked of a cross section of the community, this newspaper editor had successfully defined the life, character, and reputation of a spiritual leader in that community. I knew that, long after that man was gone, the results of his ministry would endure. He was mentoring and discipling new generations of leaders. He was living what he taught, and he was teaching others to live and lead the same way. What greater legacy could any leader leave behind?

I know of another pastor who retired after nearly three decades of ministry. He had served in three different churches, and in each church, attendance had more than doubled during his tenure. When he retired, one of his friends asked him, "What do you consider your single most important accomplishment?"

"That's easy," he replied. "It's the thirty-seven people I discipled who are today in some form of full-time Christian ministry."

He didn't point to increased church attendance, bigger church budgets, or completed building programs. His legacy was people. His legacy was leaders—thirty-seven of them over a period of nearly thirty years. What a legacy to aspire to.

Graduation Day

Every course of instruction must come to an end. Students receive diplomas and graduate. Having completed their preparation, they go out into the world and make a difference.

The disciples of Jesus had a graduation ceremony, and we read about it in John 20. Following the resurrection, Jesus appeared to his followers in the same upper room in which they had eaten the Passover meal before the crucifixion. There he delivered a commencement address that was both brief and profound: "Peace be with you. As the Father has sent me, even so I am sending you" (John 20:21).

The training was ended. The disciples were ready. So Jesus commissioned them to go out into the world and proclaim the gospel. This brings us to our final leadership principle from the life of Jesus:

Principle 18

Authentic Christlike leaders disciple others
who become leaders who disciple others.

That was the whole point of their three-year training program with Jesus. He was turning followers into leaders who would in turn recruit more followers to become leaders. Generation by generation, century by century, the church would endure and grow and change the world.

Jesus was one man, but he multiplied himself through the lives of his followers. And they in turn multiplied themselves. And their followers multiplied themselves. That's the leadership style of Jesus.

If that is your leadership style and mine, then no matter where we go, no matter what our leadership arena, no matter who we lead, we will become unstoppable.

And we will change our world.

Notes

Chapter 2: Acknowledging Those Who Have Gone Before

1. Tom Morris, "Tom Morris Quotes," ThinkExist.com, http://thinkexist.com/quotation/socrates_ had_a_student_named_plato-plato_had_a/324453.html.

2. Anonymous, "Thoughts About Life," MySeniorPortal.com, www.myseniorportal.com/cms_ contents/show_category_content/Thoughts%20about%20life/583#break.

Chapter 3: The Leader as Shepherd

1. Howard Schultz interviewed by Adi Ignatius, "The HBR Interview: 'We Had to Own the Mistakes," Harvard Business School Publishing, July 26, 2010, www.eiu.com/index .asp?layout=ebArticleVW3&article_id=597286844&channel_id=788114478&category_ id=1168152916&refm=vwCat&page_title=Article&rf=0.

2. Pat Williams, *How to Be Like Walt* (Deerfield Beach, FL: Health Communications, Inc., 2006), 114, 352.

Chapter 5: Courage

1. Richard Henry Popkin, *The History of Scepticism: From Savonarola to Bayle* (New York: Oxford University Press, 2003), 5.

Chapter 6: Gentleness

1. C.S. Lewis, *Surprised by Joy: The Shape of My Early Life* (New York: Houghton Mifflin Harcourt, 1955), 229.

Chapter 7: Generosity

1. Alison Morgan, "Business Mentoring Matters," Management Mentors, August 28, 2012, www.management-mentors.com/about/corporate-mentoring-matters-blog/bid/62174/ Statistics-on-Corporate-Mentoring.

2. Linda Taylor, "See a Need—Meet a Need," Koach Konsulting LLC, June 3, 2011, http://koach konsulting.wordpress.com/tag/mentor/.

3. Ibid.

Chapter 9: Forgiveness

1. Clifton Fadiman, *The Little, Brown Book of Anecdotes* (New York: Little, Brown, 1985), 360.

2. Reverend Stirling Gahan, "Account by Reverend H. Stirling Gahan on the Execution of Edith Cavell," Edith Cavell website, www.revdc.net/cavell/gahan.htm.

Chapter 10: Power

1. Amy Henry, *What It Takes: Speak Up, Step Up, Move Up* (New York: St. Martin's Press, 2004), 82.

2. Peter J. Frost, *Toxic Emotions at Work: How Compassionate Managers Handle Pain and Conflict* (Boston: Harvard Business Press, 2003), 37.

3. Eve Tahmincioglu, *From the Sandbox to the Corner Office: Lessons Learned on the Journey to the Top* (Hoboken: Wiley, 2006), 212.

4. Neil Cavuto, "Truett Cathy, Founder of Chick-fil-A," *Your World with Neil Cavuto*, FoxNews .com, November 12, 2002, www.foxnews.com/on-air/your-world-cavuto/2002/11/12/ truett-cathy-founder-chick-fil.

5. J. Michael Waller, "Ridicule: An Instrument in the War on Terrorism," Public Diplomacy White Paper No. 7, The Institute of World Politics, IWP.com, February 9, 2006, www.iwp.edu/ news_publications/detail/ridicule-an-instrument-in-the-war-on-terrorism.

6. Robert I. Sutton, "Are You a Jerk at Work?," *Greater Good—The Science of a Meaningful Life*, University of California at Berkeley, Winter 2007–2008, http://greatergood.berkeley.edu/article/ item/are_you_jerk_work.

Chapter 13: The Lonely Calling

1. Colin L. Powell, *My American Journey* (New York: Random House, 2003), 308.

2. Gene Edward Smith, *Eisenhower: In War and Peace* (New York: Random House, 2012), 352.

3. Ibid., 353.

Chapter 15: Criticism

1. John Eldredge, *Wild at Heart: Discovering the Secret of a Man's Soul* (Nashville: Thomas Nelson, 2001), xiii.

2. David M. Kennedy, Lizabeth Cohen, Thomas A. Bailey, *The American Pageant: A History of the American People, Vol. 1, To 1877* (Boston: Wadsworth, 2010), 212.

3. Pat Williams, *The Leadership Wisdom of Solomon: 28 Essential Strategies for Leading with Integrity* (Cincinnati: Standard Publishing, 2010), 34.

4. Ibid., 190-91.

5. Thomas Freiling, *Walking with Lincoln: Spiritual Strength from America's Favorite President* (Grand Rapids, MI: Revell, 2009), 98-99.

Chapter 16: Molehills and Mountains

1. Steve Jacobson, *Carrying Jackie's Torch: The Players Who Integrated Baseball—and America* (Chicago: Lawrence Hill Books, 2007), 217.

Chapter 17: Where Leaders Come From

1. John Maxwell, *The 21 Irrefutable Laws of Leadership Workbook: Revised and Updated* (Nashville: Thomas Nelson, 2007), 143-44.

Chapter 18: Turning Followers into Leaders

1. Pat Williams, *Coaching Your Kids to Be Leaders* (Nashville: Hachette, 2008), 206-7.

About
Michael Youssef

Dr. Michael Youssef was born in Egypt and lived in Lebanon and Australia before coming to the United States, where he fulfilled a childhood dream of becoming an American citizen. He holds theological degrees from Moore College and Fuller Theological Seminary and a doctorate in cultural anthropology from Emory University in Atlanta. He founded The Church of The Apostles, which became the launching pad for his international media ministry, Leading The Way, now reaching audiences in nearly every major city in the world.

Dr. Youssef has been teaching the Bible for more than 50 years and has authored more than 50 books, including popular titles such as *Saving Christianity?*, *Life-Changing Prayers*, *Is the End Near?*, *How to Read the Bible*, and *Heaven Awaits*. He and his wife reside in Atlanta and have four grown children and 14 grandchildren.

For more on Dr. Michael Youssef and *Leading The Way*, visit LTW.org.

Other Harvest House Books by Michael Youssef

Conquer

Fearless Living tn Troubled Times

God, Help Me Overcome My Circumstances

God, Help Me Rebuild My Broken World

God, Just Tell Me What to Do

Leading the Way Through Daniel

Leading the Way Through Ephesians

Leading the Way Through Galatians

Leading the Way Through Joshua

My Refuge, My Strength

The Leadership Style of Jesus

To learn more about Harvest House books and
to read sample chapters, visit our website:

www.HarvestHousePublishers.com

HARVEST HOUSE PUBLISHERS
EUGENE, OREGON